19434

(Treitscke, Heinrich von)
rigins of Prussianism

te Due

Origins of Prussianism

Treitschke's
Origins of Prussianism

(The Teutonic Knights)

translated by
EDEN & CEDAR
PAUL

London
George Allen & Unwin Ltd

Treitschke's
Origins of Prussianism

(The Teutonic Knights)

translated by
EDEN & CEDAR
PAUL

NEW YORK

Howard Fertig

1969

First published in English in 1942

Howard Fertig, Inc. edition 1969
Published by arrangement with George Allen & Unwin Ltd.

Library of Congress Catalog Card Number: 68-9588

Grateful acknowledgment is hereby made to the
Harvard College Library for permission to use its
copy of *Origins of Prussianism* in reproducing
the present edition of this work.

PRINTED IN THE UNITED STATES OF AMERICA
BY NOBLE OFFSET PRINTERS, INC.

The German original of this work, entitled *Das deutsche Ordensland Preussen*, was published in 1862, the year when Bismarck became minister-president of Prussia.

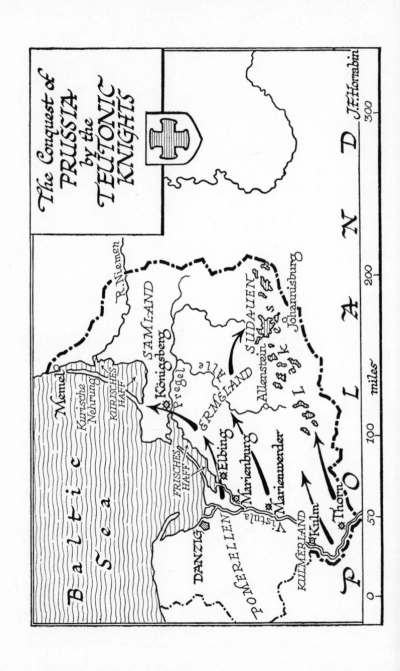

The Conquest of PRUSSIA by the TEUTONIC KNIGHTS

J.F.Horrabin

Baltic Sea

R.Niemen

Memel

Kurische Nehrung

KURISCHES HAFF

SAMLAND

Königsberg

Pregel

Alle

FRISCHES HAFF

ERMELAND

Elbing

Marienburg

Vistula

Marienwerder

DANZIG

POMERELLEN

KULMERLAND

Kulm

Thorn

Allenstein

SUDAUEN

Johannisburg

P O L A N D

0   50   100   miles   200   300

Translators' Preface

Heinrich von Treitschke, the author of this very remarkable study of the colonization of Old Prussia by the Teutonic Knights (substantially an account of the origins of Prussianism), was born at Dresden in 1834 and died at Berlin in 1896, before completing his most famous work, *History of Germany in the Nineteenth Century*, which he carried on only to 1847. That was translated into English and published here during the war of 1914–1918, in seven volumes. The present essay was penned in 1862. In youth Treitschke had liberal leanings which made it impossible for him to begin his professorial career in Saxony, and he was still unacademic when he wrote *Das deutsche Ordensland Preussen*. But his liberalism was never more than skin-deep—never "radical." Besides being an enthusiastic admirer of Prussianism, he was bitten by the antisemitism which has long been one of the curses of Germany. The fact that the two most prominent German socialists among his contemporaries in youth, Marx and Lassalle, were both of Jewish extraction, may have contributed to Treitschke's hatred of socialism. But antisemitism apart, there was enough

7

ground for dislike of national socialism, after the fashion of Lassalle, and international communism, after the fashion of Marx, in a man who idolized a "State" which should be organized to protect and further the interests and to diffuse the national "civilization" of a possessing class—with a modicum of "liberal" respect for the well-being of workers and peasants. (Of course Treitschke, who died twenty years before the recent Russian revolution, would never have phrased his Statism in any such terms.)

Still, the work here translated bears some traces of the liberalism which, in the end, Treitschke forsook, and is not entirely free from criticism of the Germans. But it exemplifies the writer's most salient characteristics: a worship of the State; belief in the fundamental excellence of the German race and of German ways (a belief which made him a forerunner of Nazism); and a conviction that, by divine dispensation, it had been the mission of the Hohenzollerns, working through Prussia, to unify Germany and ensure the unrestricted predominance of those who are now usually spoken of by Germanophils as Nordics or Aryans. What he would have thought of the second Emperor William in later days, and still more what he would have thought of Adolf Hitler, may be open to question; but the study of the late-medieval Ordensland has a strong bearing on the present war, which we will lightly touch upon after a few quotations to exemplify the points we have been making.

To explain the need for his book, Treitschke writes (p. 18): "There is hardly even an outline sketch to convey to the mind of a South German boy an intimation of the most stupendous and fruitful occurrence of the later Middle Ages—the northward and eastward rush of the German spirit and the formidable activities of our people as conqueror, teacher, discipliner of its neighbours."

He writes (p. 19) of the impossibility of understanding Germany unless one is familiar with "those pitiless racial conflicts whose vestiges . . . live on mysteriously in the habits of our people."

The Teutonic Knights (p. 20) "were not only swashbuckling soldiers, but also thoughtful administrators; not only abstemious monks, but also venturesome merchants, and (still more remarkable) bold and far-seeing statesmen."

He speaks (p. 21) of "the supreme value of the State, and of civic subordination to the purposes of the State, which the Teutonic Knights perhaps proclaimed more loudly than do any other voices speaking to us from the German past."

Here are two interesting criticisms (p. 22): "Kindliness . . . is wrongfully declared to be an essential virtue of the Germans"; and (p. 39) "the full harshness of our national spirit was displayed when conquerors endowed with the triple pride of Christians, knights, and Germans had to form front against the heathen."

Now for his views on colonization (pp. 55–56): "Thus did our people, upon this narrow stage, forestall those two main trends of colonial policy which were subsequently to guide Britain and Spain with equal success upon the vast expanses of America. In the unhappy clash between races inspired by fierce mutual enmity, the blood-stained savagery of a quick war of annihilation is more humane, less revolting, than the specious clemency of sloth, which keeps the vanquished in the state of brute beasts while either hardening the hearts of the victors or reducing them to the dull brutality of those they subjugate."

Old Prussia (in later days East Prussia), even when Germanized (and readers of this study will judge for themselves how far the Germanization may have been effected by the blood-stained savagery of a quick war of annihilation which Treitschke considers preferable to the specious clemency of sloth), still had (p. 161) "a population difficult to guide and harsh in its judgments."

His contempt for the Slavs makes him claim Copernicus as a Teuton, for he writes (p. 152) "at Frauenburg a German canon," etc., ignoring the fact that the astronomer, whose unlatinized name was

Koppernik, is usually considered to have been either a Pole or a Czech.

Foreshadowing the Empire to be established eight years later, Treitschke writes in his eloquent peroration (p. 162): "the Imperial Eagle which, through the storms of the ages, continued to wave undismayed above the forces that championed it in the distant Mark, has once again spread its pinions dominantly over German soil. He must indeed be a dullard whom the contemplation of this troubled but unceasing metamorphosis fails to inspire with the most ardent convictions. Let us encourage ourselves with history's greatest blessing, the freedom of that clear vision which enables us, amid the vicissitudes, the follies, and the sins of the moment, to recognize the inalterable dominion of world-constructing laws."

It is interesting to note that many years after those words were written the German flag (not the Imperial Eagle, indeed, but the Swastika) waves, not only in Austria, which might conceivably be regarded as "German," but in two Slav lands where Germans are few and far between, in Poland and Czecho-Slovakia.

Enough of generally illustrative quotations. We pass to a brief description of the country and the people with whose colonization the Teutonic Knights were mainly concerned, and to a few words upon the bearing of this old, old story upon the present sanguinary conflict.

At the close of the twelfth century, when the religious organization of German crusaders was founded at Acre, and even in 1225, when the Teutonic Knights' "Drang nach Osten" or "Drive to the East" began, there were few Germans, few "Nordics," settled on the southern and eastern shores of the Baltic. The inhabitants were Wends, Borussians or Prussians, Courlanders, Lithuanians, Letts, and Estonians, all using Baltic dialects and (though language is not a trustworthy criterion of race) presumably of Slav stock. Beyond Estonia, across the Gulf of Finland, lay the Land of the Waters inhabited by people of different blood and speaking a Finno-Ugrian tongue. Southward and eastward of the Baltic belt were Poles and Russians, respectively; Slavs talking variants of Old Slavonic. The Poles were Roman Catholic Christians. The Russians, though not yet unified under stress of the Mongol invasion, had been Christianized by Byzantine missionaries, and therefore belonged to the Greek Orthodox Church. The Balto-Slavs, and notably the Borussians or Old Prussians, were still pagans.

We quote Treitschke's not unsympathetic description of the last-named in the days before the Teutonic Knights' "colonization" (p. 34): "Here a Lithuanian stock (presumably mingled with peoples of other races)

had for thousands of years lived inoffensively apart. . . .
Those who were to become known as the 'German
Spartans' had hitherto dwelt tranquilly as peaceful
herdsmen and tillers of the soil, amusing themselves
during the long winter evenings by the recital of gentle
elegiac verses."

Obviously, then, they were fit objects for crusading
enthusiasm and the spread of German civilization.
But look at the map and note how this involved the
thrusting of a German wedge between Poland and the
Baltic, and, farther north, between Russia and the
Baltic; and the introduction of a Christianity which
differed from the Russian creed, and later (when
"reformed") would differ from the Polish creed. Racial
conflicts, intensified by religious zeal, would then
become inevitable. Nor has the likelihood of clashes
in this eastern cockpit of Germany (as much a "cockpit" as the western one on the Rhine) been removed by
the passing of the centuries, or by the rise of the Nazis
with their determination to revise the settlement made
at Versailles after the last Great War and the recon-
stitution of Poland.

Listen to Treitschke once more (p. 66): "Incessantly
the Polish aristocrats urged" King Casimir the Great
"to declare war against the Ordensland. How could
he possibly endure . . . that the Germans should steal his
last stretch of coast in addition to robbing him of the

lower reaches of the Vistula?" Near the close Treitschke writes (p. 158) of "the first partition of Poland," in 1772, "when the heritage of which" the Germans "had been robbed was restored to our people." Must there not result a bad case of "pull devil, pull baker," which no hocus-pocus with Polish Corridors can be expected to cure? Nor has it been cured, it has rather been aggravated, by the extension of Prussianism from Old Prussia to the Prussia of our modern atlases, by the expansion of Germanism (surely a *reductio ad absurdum*) from Germany proper to include Austria, Poland, and Czecho-Slovakia, with designs on Tirol, Rumania, Bessarabia, South Russia, Caucasia, Transcaucasia, and the oil-wells of Baku. Here we have the Drive to the East with a vengeance. Yet Treitschke can write sense about such schemes when the boot is on the other leg. For instance (p. 127): "The fanatical alliance of the Slav peoples became more stalwart than ever. On the ground that 'blood is thicker than water,' the kings of Poland entered into a league with the Hussites and the princes of Pomerania." Is not Treitschke a good example of what he himself has just called (p. 126) "the profound truth that every great man is no less richly endowed for evil than for good?"

How can this pull-devil-pull-baker business, this incessant fighting in the world's cockpits, be cured? Not by the reversal in 1914 of the defeat sustained at

Tannenberg by the Germans in 1410 at the hands of
the Slavs—and perhaps a yet further reversal after a
prolonged and devastating Blitzkrieg; not by Polish
Corridors; not by any futile attempt to re-establish
the subdivided particularist Germany of the Middle
Ages. In one way only, by the abandonment of the
outworn system of a number of independent nationalist
sovereign States, each imperialist, each endeavouring
to impose its own civilization, Nordic or otherwise, on
its neighbours. In a word, by the foundation of
Cosmopolis, as the only way of ending the Martyrdom
of Man; Cosmopolis, long overdue, often hinted at,
and, even now, almost too late. This must be a world
where a New Spirit universally prevails; a world
throughout which there has been a universal New
Deal; and a world where the peace will be kept by a
federal air-police, the only air force allowed. Utopia?
Yes, but a Utopia which has at length become practicable, as it was not yet in More's day. Practicable and
necessary, being Hobson's choice. The only alter-
natives for "homo sapiens" are Utopia or Annihilation.

But how can we reach Utopia? Read Treitschke's
enthralling account of the colonization of Old Prussia
by the Teutonic Knights, and think for yourselves.
Ponder what he writes (p. 150) about that which
took place in the Ordensland when the power of the

Germans had been superseded by that of the Poles, how "the country suffered greatly from the Poles' shiftiness," and how "the foundations of decent human behaviour were undermined"; ask yourselves what has been going on in the same region since the end of August, 1939, and whether any form of fanatical nationalism or racialism, German, Polish, or other, is likely to lay the foundations of decent human behaviour. Ponder, above all, his concluding sentence, with which we shall end this preface, though perhaps we do not mean precisely what Treitschke meant when he wrote it (p. 161): "Let us encourage ourselves with history's greatest blessing, the freedom of that clear vision which enables us, amid the vicissitudes, the follies, and the sins of the moment, to recognize the inalterable dominion of world-constructing laws."

LONDON,   EDEN AND CEDAR PAUL.
  July, 1941.

The Origins of Prussianism

One who wishes to measure the age of a people will be mistaken if he seeks to do so by numbering the years of its existence; he will find a better approach by way of the more abstruse question, what portion of the past continues to live as history in the soul of this people. Whoever, witnessing the contemporary [1862] struggle anent the fundamental structure of the German State, fails to understand that this old country of ours is now growing up for the second time, may nevertheless recognize the youth of our people in the light of something vain to deny—that the Middle Ages are infinitely remote from the consciousness of latter-day Germans. Not only have the masses wellnigh forgotten all that preceded the days of Gustavus Adolphus and the Reformation; even persons of culture will be found to entertain very few well-grounded opinions concerning the phenomena of that momentous earlier epoch. The dispute about the Empire, now again grown fierce— would it be possible in a people whose development had been simple, straightforward, and uninterrupted? Nay more, the extent of our general information with regard to the German Middle Ages is amazingly scanty, seeing that we are usually well-informed, and that we have plenty of diligent historians. What is mostly taught us by experts consists of an arbitrary hotch-potch of trivial facts which are dignified with the name of the history of the fatherland; and in conjunction therewith the story of the Holy Roman Empire which has vanished like a Midsummer Night's Dream, the story which (for all its glories) discloses the Germans to be still nothing more than learners of the alphabet. There is hardly even an outline sketch to convey to the mind of a South German boy an intimation of the most stupendous and fruitful occurrence of the later Middle Ages—the northward and eastward rush of the German spirit and the formidable activities of our people as conqueror, teacher, discipliner of its neighbours.

A happier generation than ours, growing out of the work of our own days, will perhaps come to regard as a precious blessing that which we, whose community-life is inchoate, still find it hard to value: that the Germans are so much at one with their history, as to be simultaneously very old and very young, with the result that our early days, our days of long, long ago, are not a burden on our shoulders, as aforetime the greatness of Rome was a heavy burden to the Latin nations. Prussia, more especially, may pride itself upon the name which envious rivals scornfully bestow on it, the name of upstart among the powers. For we should do well to let our eyes rest longer than we of Southern and Central Germany are wont to do upon that tangled process of development which preceded the brief two centuries of the modern history of Prussia. A vigorous sense of security rises in our hearts when we perceive how the work which has so suddenly ripened had the way prepared for it by many centuries of arduous toil. We can laugh at malicious talk about the haphazard origin of the Prussian State when we discern how modern Germany as a great power is firmly established upon the very soil on which was erstwhile upbuilded what was a New Germany to our forefathers, the Baltic great power of the Middle Ages. Who can understand the innermost nature of the Prussian people and the Prussian State unless he has familiarized his mind with those pitiless racial conflicts whose vestiges, be we aware of them or not, live on mysteriously in the habits of our people. A spell rises from the ground which was drenched with the noblest German blood in the fight on behalf of the name of Germany and the most sublime gifts of mankind.

Learned investigators have never failed to note the most stimulating episodes of this early phase in our history, the history of Old Prussia, the Ordensland colonized by the Teutonic Knights. Who that is endowed with a clear or eager imagination can fail to be allured by the thought of the wonderful strong-holds of this Brotherhood with their refectories bathed in the light of dawn and their obscure underground passages? He wants to understand these enigmatic champions, who were not only swashbuckling soldiers, but also thoughtful administrators; not only abstemious monks, but also venturesome merchants, and (still more remarkable) bold and far-seeing statesmen. Especially attractive is the thought of the statesmen: the story of a rough aristocracy which drew most of its strength from an alliance with the burgherdom; of a religious community which was as masterful towards the Church as was any temporal potentate in history; of a State which seems almost visionary, like a world that has sunk beneath the waves, so anachronistic in the way it foreshadowed the rationalistic sobriety of modern statecraft; of a colony which cannot be fitted into any theory of colonialism, and nevertheless typically fulfilled the destiny of all colonial systems in its breathless rise and its sudden fall. We are here presented with a history which at one moment produces a sinister impression by the sorrowful narrowness of its provincial particularism, and at the next uplifts the mind with wide vistas upon historical entanglements; a history no less complicated, no less involved, than our ancient escutcheon, with its one-headed eagle which one of the Hohenstaufen Emperors allowed the

Grand Master of the Order to adopt, so that it was blazoned in the remote possessions of the Teutonic Knights after the Empire itself had abandoned the emblem—and it was destined at long last to be revived as a symbol of promise by the great German State of modern times. But what thrills us inhabitants of petty German particularist States even more in the history of the Ordensland than its romantic charm, is the profound doctrine of the supreme value of the State, and of civic subordination to the purposes of State, which the Teutonic Knights perhaps proclaimed more loudly and clearly than do any other voices speaking to us from the German past.

By the time when the epoch of Protestant fervour had begun in Old Prussia, even then the old Ordensland and the State founded by the Teutonic Knights had been wellnigh forgotten: or in a spirit of fanatical rivalry their picture was caricatured and distorted by Polish priests full of national hatred; by the learned municipal historians of Danzig inspired with urban pride; and later by Kotzebue and Co. under the spell of the self-complacency characteristic of the Enlightenment. The door had also been opened to the Lapps with their love of fable. The early chroniclers of the Order lacked talent for a vivid description of character —this lack being usual in the writers of epics. Indeed, as was appropriate to the ultra-aristocratic spirit of the Teutonic Knights, such historians deliberately renounced the attempt to put the great statesmen in the limelight. When we come to modern authors, how could we expect them to escape their natural tendency to personify mighty actions? Johannes Voigt, at length, became the founder of the scientific study of history in Old Prussia, when, close upon fifty years ago, he began to compile his *Geschichte von Preussen* from the archives of the Order. To-day we can easily censure the work for its defects: for an unattractive style, a deficient criticism of the sources, the want of a broad-minded political outlook, and especially the enthusiastic stressing of beauties (this last trait being obviously the outcome of the delight of a pioneer in discovery, and of the vapid idealism of those early days of the romantic movement). We of a younger generation, having grown sceptical, cannot but laugh from time to time at these many noble and Arthurian Knights, whose deeds speak for themselves. Indeed, a considerable part of their greatness resulted from their utter lack of that kindliness which is wrongfully declared to be an essential virtue of the Germans. Nevertheless the excellent Voigt did an imperishable service. This is most plainly shown by the vigour with which, since the publication of the aforesaid history of Prussia, all classes in the eastern province have devoted themselves to the study of its early growth. A touching affection for the native land, which is perhaps more in evidence among the Old Prussians than in any other part of Germany, makes them thoroughly enjoy historical research, which went on inconspicuously throughout the years when the castle of Marienburg was being restored. The upshot has been countless monographs and symposia—which often display an unfortunate deficiency of historical discrimination. Not until recently, when Töppen, in his *Geschichte der preussischen Historiographie* (1853), subjected the old chronicles of the country to close scrutiny, did another complete change ensue in views of the early days of Prussia. The admirable collection of the sources of Prussian history (*Scriptores Rerum Prussicarum*) issued by Hirsch, Töppen, and Strehlke has paved the way for an account of Old Prussia that can conform with the strict demands of modern science. As yet no such work has been written. All I aspire to give here, in as vigorous a way as is compatible with a thumbnail sketch, is an unpretentious outline of the development of the Ordensland.

The glorious days of old German chivalry were drawing to a close. Yet once again, more splendidly than ever, was the flower of German aristocracy to bloom when forty thousand knights assembled round their hero, the ageing Frederick Barbarossa, who held his imperial court at Mainz, gave his sons "the honour-

conferring blow," and himself actually splintered a
lance in the jousts. This was in 1184. Only three
years were to elapse (so closely did decay succeed the
culminating flourish of the gala phase of the knighthood) before the Emperor, despite his love for the
chivalric order, was to lay the axe at its root by conferring upon it the suicidal "right of feud." Three
years more, and this most famous representative of
German knighthood was himself to perish miserably by
drowning or chill in the River Cydnus. Thus unhappily
opened the Third Crusade. But in the same sinister
epoch when Redbeard went to his doom, was founded
the Teutonic Order of St. Mary's Hospital at Jerusalem
—a posthumous child of the old German chivalry.
When the Latins were besieging Acre, wealthy merchants from Lübeck and Bremen took pity on their
sick fellow countrymen and sheltered them in tents
made of sail-cloth. Thus did German knights provide
for the wounded the same pious care that the "Kelts"
(the French, the Spanish, and the Italians) had long
been accustomed to receive from the Templars and
the Hospitallers. When Acre fell, the new Order was
definitively established, annexed a previously existing
hospice for the Germans in Jerusalem, and made its
headquarters in the newly conquered city (1190 to
1191). Thus significantly did German burghers stand
by the cradle of the new-born Order of Teutonic

Knights at the very moment when the equites in their arrogance were striving to deny the burghers the right to bear arms; and while its greatness lasted, the Order persisted day after day in praying for the welfare of the pious citizens of Lübeck and Bremen who had helped to found it. Even as throughout the period of the Crusades, during the great interchange of ideas between ourselves and Latin Christendom, our people continued to receive more than it gave, so was the new Order fashioned after the "Keltic" model. It owed its military organization to the Templars, its rules for the care of the sick and its spiritual discipline to the Hospitallers. But whereas the Templars were soon to undergo moral degeneration and the Hospitallers (being wardens of the Latin marches) were to lead a fitful existence in conflict with the Turks, the Teutonic Knights were speedily to outsoar their predecessors and rivals. Much longer than these did the Teutons remain exempt from the moral corruption of the East. Having more national pride than the Templars and the Hospitallers, the Teutonic Knights would from the outset accept those recruits only to whom German was a mother tongue; and soon, like Pallas born fully armed from the head of Zeus, there emerged from the head of the Grand Master the great idea of establishing a State.

For a generation it seemed that the Order, in which

as yet there could be hardly more than two hundred members, might live the aimless life of adventurers in the border regions between eastern and western civilization. It drilled and led the newly constituted infantry of the crusaders, acquiring with the sword, assisted by pious endowments, many fine estates in the Holy Land and in Greece, still more in Sicily, and a few in Germany. Amid such homeless activities, it remained shrewdly devoted to the Holy See, with the result that the Curia protected "its favourite sons" when jealous princelings quarrelled with their insubordinate and awkward subjects. In such circumstances the offended clergy forbade any attempt to take legal proceedings against the Order, and exhorted the Templars to tolerate the Teutonic Knights' wearing of a white habit, which was sufficiently differentiated by a black cross. In the history of the Order, the first mark of distinction comes with the appointment of Hermann von Salza as Grand Master. Having passed his early years in Thuringia, in a period when Christo-Germanic poesy was beginning to flourish at the Wartburg which was so friendly to minnesinging [the songs of love], he subsequently enjoyed the benefits of secular education at the imperial court of Palermo, where Frederick II, who treated him as a friend, initiated him into world-embracing schemes of imperial statecraft. He made acquaintance with the reasonable principles of that quasi-modern absolutism which the Hohenstaufen ruler had seen successfully at work among the Saracens and had introduced into his Sicilian home. The State here practised multifarious activities hitherto unknown to the Germanic world. A numerous and well-trained body of officials developed every possible method of fiscal policy, while a codified system of legislation held all under strict control. But though he was in close proximity to this "Keltic" [semi-Italian] Emperor, surrounded by Saracen bodyguards and frivolous southern poets, Salza remained German through and through. Whilst the strongly intellectual ruler attended by a train of sceptical men of learning was disposed to scoff at Christian dogmas, the faith of the Grand Master remained untarnished, his behaviour irreproachable. This man with an able, unrivalled mind knew well how to hold a balance between the contending powers of the Empire and the Church, and how to make a good use of both in order to promote the greatness of his Order. He travelled across Germany that he might persuade Valdemar, King of the Danes, to renounce any claim on Holstein, and he appeased the disaffected towns of Lombardy. Later he promoted a reconciliation between Pope and Emperor, and was the only man of note present at Anagni when the two potentates came to terms.

Such services made him seem indispensable. The

Emperor overwhelmed him with favours and granted him the right to blazon the single-headed black imperial eagle upon the shield placed over the centre of the cross worn by the Grand Master. But how, in his frequent sojourns at Acre, could so clear-sighted a statesman fail to become aware that the Order's grip upon its possessions in the East was being weakened, and that Christendom was losing its taste for the previously fostered campaign on behalf of the recovery of the Holy Land? Beyond question he must already have conceived the plan to give the Teutonic Knights a safe home in Europe. In view of the lack of controverting evidence, we are certainly entitled to believe that this glorious scheme must have been Salza's. He was glad, therefore, to send a troop of his knights when King Andreas of Hungary implored the powerful aid of the Order against the Kuman invasion, offering as guerdon the lovely Bürzen district in south-eastern Transylvania (Kronstadt and its environs). The knights were sent, and Hermann asked the Pope to declare this Hungarian fief part of St. Peter's patrimony—thus exhibiting for the first time the spirit of purposive strength and the relentless determination to pursue self-interest that were thenceforward to characterize the policy of the Teutonic Knights. But the King of Hungary was eager to rid himself quickly of his dangerous allies. Scarcely had

regret for the failure of this somewhat overbold
endeavour subsided, when there came to the Grand
Master (then negotiating with the communes of
Lombardy upon something of moment to the Emperor)
an embassy from a Polish princeling who begged
help against the Prussian pagans (1226). Thereupon
the Order began its great Christo-Germanic Crusade,
incited thereto by an Emperor who was neither
Christian nor German by sentiment. Thus on its very
threshold do we encounter the secret inveracity of the
State of the Teutonic Knights. Its campaign for the
conversion of the heathen was opened in days when
the simple faith of earlier times had already begun to
grow cold.

At the beginning of the thirteenth century, forsooth,
the omens were unpropitious for the founding of a
chivalric State. Throughout the European continent
the foundations of the old knighthood were crumbling.
Again and again the German nobility was refusing
to undertake expeditions to Italy, for it had already
grown weary of the picturesque statecraft of its old
Emperor. Silent, now, were the halls of the Wartburg,
where minnesinging had once resounded so
abundantly; and in Austria, likewise, with the dying
out of the Babenbergs, knightly love-songs had ceased
to be fashionable. After a transient reprieve, the graces
of the ancient chivalric culture vanished completely

during the troublous times of the imperial interregnum, and it was with utter indifference that the equites listened when a foreign poet asked them how the Germans could bear to go on living while Conradin remained unavenged. The more cultivated French noblesse, too, had degenerated in consequence of the atrocities that characterized the Albigensian wars. Nevertheless there appeared in Saint Louis a brilliant representative of the good old days—a man who was a true knight as well as a worthy king. But after fourteen years he was succeeded on the throne by Philip the Fair, a cold calculator who opened a rougher and more modern epoch. At the same date, in England, amid severe birth-pangs, the Lower House was born. Now had begun the century of the three Edwards which, romantic though it was, bore in its vitals the germs of latter-day English political life. With the manners and customs of the old chivalry there disappeared, no less, the corresponding artistic forms— the distinguished charm of the late Romance style. But new growths sprang up rapidly from the fertile soil of this richly endowed generation. In Rome originated sinister plants, the Inquisition and the mendicant orders. In this north of ours, by the close of the twelfth century a new development was in progress, less brilliant perhaps than the policy of the Hohenstaufens, but more lasting and steadfast—the great phase of tuition for the aggressive forces of our people. Long ere this the Franks had amalgamated the German spirit with the classical civilization and Christianity. Now the Saxons were to transport these Frankish achievements eastward. When Henry the Lion and Albert the Bear crushed the Wends, and when Arkona's ancient castle and temple was stormed by the Danes and the mysterious sanctuary of the Slav god Suantevit was destroyed by the Christians, then German burghers and peasants, impelled by the longing for freedom, the pressure of over-population, the force of the sea, or simple venturesomeness, moved eastward into the devastated regions.

Devoid of understanding, because immersed in Italian affairs, were the Emperors as they watched this great dispensation. At Christmas 1244, indeed, Frederick II actually bestowed upon the Danish Kings all the land beyond the Elbe and the Elde. Thus was forced upon northern Germany the policy to which it has ever since been faithful. Without help from the Empire, and often in defiance of the Empire's commands, it worked on its own to enlarge the Empire. The burghers of Low-Germany took action, defeating the Danes at Bornhöved; and in 1234 Lübeck won its first seafight off Warnemünde. Rapidly now, though nature favoured them little on a coast poorly supplied with harbours, the burghers multiplied their strength.

The mighty gifts of German civilization—the sword, the heavy plough, the masonry and the "free-giving air" of the cities, together with the rigid discipline of the Church—were imposed upon the easy-going inhabitants of the east. The trading centres of Scandinavia became German. All the mercantile energies of the north were masterfully exploited by German burghers who, while excluding immigrants of other races, vigorously battled to keep open for themselves these gateways into the foreign world. None but German merchants might set foot upon the inhospitable soil of Russia; and since, in these lawless times, the merchants must brave the hardships of the journey, must buy and sell in person, they went as far as the trading republic of Novgorod, the chief market for the valuable peltry of the north. To the German burghers accrued the heritage of the Wends, sea-power in the Baltic; and concurrently with the Hanseatic League there developed the burgher triumphs of Gothic architecture. In the course of the century, the very dominions of the Slav petty princes of Pomerania and Silesia passed under the control of German culture. Even Poland, whose claims to sovereignty had once extended to the Harz, having now been speedily reduced in power by internal disputes, succumbed to the victorious march of German civilization. The influence of German free municipal institutions spread to Sandomir and Cracow, and German cities sprang to life wherever there were ecclesiastical or manorial institutions. Of the inhabitants of Poland, none but the nobles were led by a sound national instinct to resist these ill-omened developments. The only advantage they took of the encroachments of the aforesaid free municipal institutions of Germany was to shake off royal jurisdiction and to fix upon the masses of ill-treated peasants (regarded as having no rights) the yoke of a so-called "free seigniority" of the Polish aristocracy. But German colonists moved farther east than Poland. Some Low German merchants who, with the boldness of those days, were coasting north-eastward in little river-boats, had to take refuge from a storm in the estuary of the Dvina. Thereupon the great bishop Albert of Buxhövden, in alliance with German burghers and the Teutonic Knights, subjugated far-off Livonia; and soon there came into being as German towns the favourite "neophytes" of the Hanseatic League: Reval, Dorpat, and, before all, Riga (1201), which adopted into its escutcheon a modification of the arms of Hamburg and Bremen—towers from the former and keys from the latter.

To this mighty chain of German colonies encircling the Baltic, one link was wanting; Prussia eastward of the Vistula. Safeguarded against Slav and Byzantine-

Christian influence by an endless chain of marshes along the Dnieper, Dniester, and Pripet, a Lithuanian stock (presumably mingled with peoples of other races) had for thousands of years lived inoffensively apart. Just as to-day the Baltic has less influence than other seas upon its hinterland, so there, where long strips of land and the widely extended lagoons or "haffs" that lay behind the narrow promontories hindered access to the high sea; and though there was considerable exchange of goods between this townless folk and some of the seaports to the west of them, the trade had no influence worth considering upon their manners and customs.   A semi-secret priesthood, whose members were rarely seen by their co-nationals and never by strangers, fostered consecrated serpents in shrines made of oak-branches, while keeping alight on stone altars the odoriferous amber-fires kindled in honour of the gods of a faith that bore few traces of the usual characteristics of primitive religions—such as blood-thirstiness and sexual orgies.   Those who were to become known as the "German Spartans" had hitherto dwelt tranquilly as peaceful herdsmen and tillers of the soil, amusing themselves during the long winter evenings by the recital of gentle elegiac verses. They were split up into a number of petty communities, and had no desire for the arduous political labour that is requisite to overcome the separateness, the particularism, natural to ill-developed tribes. But they were free people, settled where they had been since time immemorial, protected on the western side by the boggy basin of the Vistula, southward by powerful abatis, huge lakes, and thick forests, all of which were alarming to the would-be invader. The Poles had had many reasons to know this. Again and again Kulmerland, the frontier province which separated them from Prussia, had been ruthlessly laid waste by the enraged heathen. Stubbornly did the Prussians cling to their ancient faith. As early as the tenth century Adalbert the Czech, bishop of Prague (ultimately to be revered as patron saint of Prussia), was slain by the furious Prussians when he impiously entered the sacred wood of Romove. Soon afterwards was killed Bruno, the Saxon prince, the first German Christian to penetrate this inhospitable land with missionary intent, and to offer up his blood for his religion. Now, in the beginning of the thirteenth century, Christian of Oliva near Danzig, a Cistercian monk, resumed the attempt, founding the first Christian church beyond the Vistula, and was thereupon made bishop of Prussia by the Pope. The Blessed Virgin, who was considered guardian of the coasts far along the Baltic where fisheries thrived, was also to control the land beside the Frisches Haff. The Curia took this heathen country under its special protection as a field of instruction, in accordance with that seemingly self-evident right which civilized nations have always claimed as against barbarians, and one which in accordance with the doctrines of Christianity indubitably accrued to the Holy See. But as soon as the new bishop, in league with Duke Conrad of Masovia, led a crusade into the territory which was to be converted, the Prussians flamed up in revolt, extirpated all traces of Christian settlement, and spread fire and slaughter into the Polish duke's domains. The duke, recking little of the anarchical spirit of the Poles and of the fact that they were by no means ripe for Christianity, decided upon summoning to his aid the Germans, who were arch enemies of Poland.

Hermann von Salza agreed to help, but the crusading armies of the Teutonic Knights were not to come as auxiliary troops. The plan of founding a State for the Order was now ripening. The Emperor was easily induced to grant the religious warriors Kulmerland and all future conquests in Prussia, with full jurisdiction and lordship. This was in 1226. Then, in 1230, Conrad of Masovia was persuaded to cede Kulmerland formally to the Order. Finally, in 1234, the Grand Master moved the Pope to declare the territory to be an appanage of St. Peter and lease it to the Knights for a moderate annual rent payable to the Curia. Thus came about forthwith Prussia's dubious position in relation to the German realm, which was to have such dire consequences. But another result was that a German State was thrust between the Poles and the sea, with consequent perpetual enmity between Poland and that State. Of course the charters gave no warrant for the contention that the foundation of the State of the Teutonic Knights infringed the rights of Bishop Christian and Duke Conrad. But it remains obvious that the interests of the pair were nowise compatible with the far-reaching plans of the Order. It was impossible that the bishop could wish to pass beneath the suzerainty of the Knights' State, seeing that near by in Livonia the Order was subject to the archbishop of Riga. Still less could the Polish duke desire to see a German State established between himself and the Baltic. As the charters disclose, it was hesitatingly and in the utmost need that he surrendered Kulmerland, which was now to be the starting-point of the German policy of conquest. In the very year of the papal gift the support which at first the Poles had given to the Order was withdrawn. They were beginning to realize that political and national oppositions outweighed community of religion. It was only local dissensions superadded to the instability of barbaric aims that withheld them from the obviously natural course of declaring open war against the Order.

The Curia now set all the levers of clerical authority to work in order to ensure that the Order of St. Mary should achieve the conquest of this heathen country. The Cross was preached throughout the Empire. Whoever took part in the Crusade—even the Ghibellines, who had been accused of arson and of maltreating the clergy—would have all his sins forgiven; and the Pope willingly approved the annulment of the marriages of men who desired "to enter the period of salvation under the new Maccabees." Now came the time when the papacy reached the climax of temporal power: for it was able, in Portugal, to depose a king who surrendered without striking a blow; in Iceland, to suppress a republic that had lasted four centuries; in Germany, to declare the choice of a monarch invalid if it lacked papal approval. Since in any case a crusade was advantageous to clerical authority, Rome might well hope that in the newly acquired territories its legates would hold unrestricted power among the members of an Order that was ringed by enemies. In the year 1231, Hermann Balke, the provincial appointed by Salza, crossed the Vistula with his crusading army and seven brethren of the Order; and there now began a steady and carefully planned advance, unique in these days of irregular warfare. The instant any region had been occupied by the Germans, German ships would bring beams and blocks of stone down the Vistula, with the result that there promptly arose fortified cities whose happily chosen site is still a marvel to strategic experts. The first were Thorn, Kulm, and Marienwerder. . . . These advanced posts were on a small scale what the Ordensland, the settlement of the Teutonic Knights, became on a large scale for the German realm; a breakwater thrusting from the German shore boldly into the wave-tost sea of the eastern peoples. Thus were gained new stepping-stones for a further advance, the gaze of the barbarians being diverted from the previous conquests; and since the Prussians were compelled to gather in full force against these strongholds, the mounted Germans escaped the dangers of petty warfare which would have led to their inevitable destruction in a land of forests and marshes.

With the usual incapacity of barbarians for taking the future into account, the Prussians began by tolerating the erection of these unfamiliar fortresses. But the situation grew clear to them by degrees, until their slumbering savagery burst forth, and warfare of inhuman cruelty ensued. The full harshness of our own national spirit was displayed when conquerors endowed with the triple pride of Christians, Knights, and Germans had to form front against the heathen. The romantic stimulus of these struggles was intensified by the wild though stately poesy of the north. Welcome were the frosts that prepared hard ways through the otherwise impenetrable forests which were trackless in a mild winter. Often under the weird glitter of the Northern Lights combat was joined upon the ice that covered the rivers and the marshes, until the solid crust broke beneath the weight of the warriors and the men of both sides were engulfed to their chilly doom. Since the Prussians were disintegrated both politically and militarily, they had to yield in the end to the strongly organized German minority; and after the first great victory (Sirguna, 1234) there was to be heard again and again the proud and exultant song of the invaders:

> Let us all show joy of heart,
> For lo the heathen feel the smart.

Six years later the first great insurrection of the subjugated was pitilessly repressed. More and more frequently were venturesome German nobles lured by the rumour of such victories to join the campaign against Prussia. Otakar, king of Bohemia and duke of Austria, was one of those who joined in the Prussian campaign, and saga has adorned the story of his expedition with a wealth of wondrous exploits. After the Frisches Haff and the channel of the Vistula had been won, and safeguarded by the fortress of Elbing, the Order prepared for the conquest of Samland, the core of heathen territory. The wood of Romove, the venerable holy of holies, was taken; the sacred oaks were felled by the axes of Christian priests, and the most exalted of the Samland nobles was christened by the name of the king of Bohemia—Otakar, who, with Slav disregard for truth, claimed to have baptized the whole population of Samland, and to have extended Bohemia from the Adriatic to the Baltic. But amid these fantastic vauntings, the Order's sober military statecraft remained unmodified; for the system of advanced posts was pushed forward steadily. Even before the annexation of Samland was accomplished, the Teutonic Knights sent troops and villeins eastward over the Kurische Nehrung, to found Memelburg. In honour of their royal guest, a fortress was built in Samland. It was called Königsberg, and a knight with a crowned helmet figured in its coat of arms (1255). In like manner the Ascanian margrave Otto III, who was Otakar's comrade-at-arms, granted the new fortress of Brandenburg-am-Haff the right of including his red eagle in its escutcheon.

The ambitions of the youthful militarist State were more expansive. It aspired to the command of the Baltic. As early as 1237 the Livonian Brethren of the Sword amalgamated with the Teutonic Knights. Thus two years before his death Hermann von Salza was able to enjoy the fact that his Order, so recently still homeless, claimed and actually held a long strip of coastland. But what so radically differentiated this campaign of our German seigniors from the trivial greed of ordinary mounted adventurers was the faithful alliance between the crusaders and the burgherdom. Although it may well be presumed that to begin with the plans of the Teutonic Knights went no further than a design to treat the province as Christendom treated its conquests in the East, they proposed (when they had annexed the territory) to use it on behalf of their own political and religious aims, and though most of the crusaders had been accustomed to return to their homes after a year's campaigning—the tough resistance of the infuriated Prussians compelled the Germans to pour their forces into the lands to be acquired. The burghers of Low Germany were summoned to Prussia, a town became established close to the walls of every important stronghold built by the Knights, and soon in Prussia no less than in Silesia resounded the song of the German settlers: "In God's good name we march." In the Charter of Kulm (1233) the Order magnanimously granted the new settlers the privileges of the Magdeburg Right which ever since have accrued to the majority of Prussian towns. It even allowed the burghers of Lübeck, when they founded an offshoot at Elbing, to arrange matters there as they pleased. Having granted such favours, the Teutonic Knights could later, when in difficulties, confidently apply to the burghers of the Hanseatic League, "who have so often besprinkled this field of the faith with their blood." Since there was this core of German civilization in the cities and the castles, it could not prove difficult to keep the open countryside under control. Surely it would be enough that churches should be built at every turn, that villages where there was a relapse to the worship of the old gods should be ruthlessly burned, and that the children of the Prussian nobles should be educated in convent schools? The Letts and other Balts who were Slav neighbours to the east and to the west speedily became aware of what the German colonization portended. Duke Suantepolk of Pomerania, a Christian magnate who was lord on the left bank of the Vistula, often joined forces with the heathen Prussians, Cours, and Lithuanians. Soon it became a shrewd principle of Lithuanian statecraft to evade imminent destruction by undergoing baptism, with a firm determination to resume the old faith as soon as the peril was over. Nevertheless though such struggles were unceasing, by the year 1260 the ownership of Prussia seemed to have passed definitively to the Order.

But the Order had again to fight for its conquest, nay for its very existence. The vanquished murmured against the outrageous insolence of those who, while carrying off Prussian children to be brought up in convent schools, were fiercely opposed to intermarriage with persons that were not of pure German descent. Even the clergy did not trouble to learn the native language of their converts; and in the words and actions of the German priests all that the Prussian could understand was the scorn manifested for the old sanctities. But when the Germans themselves did not dare to enter the uncanny shrines of evil spirits or to set up their dwellings in the groves of the pagan gods, it was natural enough that no Samlander could be persuaded to plough the earth between the sacred trees of Romove. It was through the strangers that the people who had no State first became acquainted with the heavy sacrifices and grievous burdens imposed by genuine political life. The Prussians had to build fortresses and undertake militia duties against their fellow-tribesmen. The furtive malice that ensued from slavery introduced new and most undesirable character-traits into the composition of a people which had heretofore been innocent and harmless. "A Prussian will betray his master," says the German proverb. No Prussian might hand a German a tankard without having previously sampled the contents. During the summer nights of the year 1261 a mysterious life stirred in the Prussian forests. A chief priest appeared among the heathen conspirators, and from the tops of the ancient oaks the voice of the old gods announced that the hour for vengeance had struck. The movement was headed by Prussian noblemen, who had been trained in German convent schools, who were accustomed to German discipline, and were ready to slay the master with his own weapons. The savage bailiff of the Teutonic Knights thereupon invited to Lenzenberg on the Frisches Haff a number of suspect Prussian aristocrats—and set fire to the place over their heads. The exasperating news spread swiftly through the country, with the result that by September the whole populace had taken up arms, to burn the blockhouses of the Order and kill those who were building them. Terrible was the danger to the Germans, even worse than the risk of annihilation by the Tartars which the country had only escaped thanks to a fortunate chance twenty years before. The Landmaster of Livonia was totally defeated by the Lithuanians, Courland regained its liberty, and the Wendish princes of the west were eager to send help against the detested German invaders. All the horrors of the previous wars pale when compared with those of this struggle. According to one story, the captured Teutonic magnate, clad in his triple armour, was roasted to death as an offering to Thor; according to another version, having been nailed to a tree with a spike thrust through his navel, he was pitilessly flogged until his eviscerated body collapsed.

After ten years, when German dominion had been almost destroyed, fresh victories were won for the Order by the stalwart Landmarshal, Conrad von Thierberg, of whom unfortunately little is known beyond his name; and in another decade, thanks to slaughter, incendiarism, and devastation, the suzerainty of the Teutons was re-established. For, though the barbarians had been apt to learn discipline and skill in the use of arms from their conquerors, they had failed to grasp the one thing needful, the conduct of a unified campaign on an extended front. The struggle went on longest in the south-eastern territory then known as Sudauen, where beside lakes and amid huge forests was settled a thriving population with many mounted aristocrats who had been hardened in the chase of aurochses, bears, and elks. At length in 1283 Skurdo, the last chieftain of the Sudauers, aided by his trusty followers, laid his own lands waste, and migrated to the still heathen Lithuania. The region he forsook bears to-day the traces of the devastation he wrought, for the great wilderness of Johannisburg now extends where the comfortable villages of the pagans were once abundant. Thus after half a century did the last of the Prussians (in the words of the chroniclers) "bow their stubborn necks beneath the faith and the Brethren"—at the very time when Courland, too, had been regained by the Order.

Taught by the disasters they had endured, the
Teutonic Knights instituted a new and harsher policy
towards those whom they had subjugated. Whereas
Prussia had hitherto been extolled as "the augmenta-
tion, protective wall, and strong buckler of the
Christian faith," it henceforward deserved the name
of the New Germany. The conquest was safeguarded
by many recent fortifications, and especially by Samland, the chief link between the northern provinces
and the southern. All the rights of the Prussians had
been forfeited in consequence of their rebellion. There
were no more treaties of peace to be made with the
vanquished; only subjugation and amnesty on terms
which varied with the magnitude of their offences and
were dictated by strategic considerations. Most of the
Prussian nobles were reduced to the level of serfs,
whereas the German peasants and those Prussians who
had continued faithful to the Teutonic overlords (even
though they had been Prussian serfs) were granted
ample privileges. Entire villages were transferred to
regions where they would be less dangerous. The last
of the Sudauers were forced to deforest the sacred
groves of Romove in Samland, which no Samlander
dared touch, and its original site is now known as the
Sudauen Nook. In this way all connexion with the
previous conditions was cut off, and a few isolated
risings were easily suppressed. Just as the State

founded by the Teutonic Knights seems to us as a whole to be nothing other than a belated "Mark," planned like Charlemagne's "Marches" for conquest, so were the duties imposed upon the conquered designed to subserve this highest function of the State. Speaking generally the burdens laid upon the peasants were not oppressive—except for the almost universal obligation to serve in the Order's militia and participate in the campaigns undertaken by the Brethren. Only the German "Kölmer" (burghers with exceptional privileges) and a small number of faithful Prussians were exempt from the hated exaction of answering the call for foreign military service; but even they had to take up arms in defence of the "fatherland," had to assemble prepared to fight when the "war-cry," spreading from village to village, announced that invasion was imminent. In accordance with the vigorous centralization that prevails in militarist States, these duties were imposed without qualification throughout the countryside. No German territorial magnate in this region might grant his underlings any rights other than those enjoyed by the serfs of the Order. That the awareness of unconditional dependence might remain unimpaired, the Teutonic Knights, who by the Pope's gift had become exclusive owners of the country, hardly ever gave their Prussian subjects title-deeds to land. But this rigid control did not suffice. It was likewise necessary to stimulate the extensive immigration of German peasants as settlers, and such settlement was actively fostered. The villages thus inaugurated soon grew into towns. At the very time when in the Empire the Emperor and the princes were stupidly trying to curtail the liberty of the German burghers, the Order granted freedom of movement to those who dwelt in its towns. There was no objection to this, since the rights of the State were always preserved. No autonomy was tolerated, and any change in municipal government needed the approval of the bailiff, an official of the Teutonic Knights.

No less masterful was the Order in its attitude towards the power of the Church. As a spiritual brotherhood it did not merely enjoy the plenitude of spiritual energy and political experience that had made the Church the supreme cultural force of the Middle Ages; it was also spared irritating friction with the Church. Outside Old Prussia the Church was either supreme or else was a hostile neighbour; in Prussia alone was it nothing but a constituent of the State. Everywhere else negotiations between the State authority and the Roman See were conducted through the instrumentality of the clergy, whereas the Old Prussian clergy could only treat with the Pope through the Order. In the Ordensland, likewise, it redounded to the advantage of the Teutonic Knights that there was no trace of the wrongfully extolled organic evolution of medieval life. Here, rather, an all-pervading will arranged things equably, however tangled their roots. One-third of the land became the property of the four bishoprics, but even on this episcopal land the territorial laws prevailed over the rights of the peasantry and the townsmen, and the universal obligation to militia service was in force. Any further acquisition of estates by the Church was prohibited. The archbishopric of the Teutonic Knights' dominions was in Riga—this dangerous power, which continued to claim suzerainty on the Western Dvina, being wisely excluded from Prussia. Just as within itself the Order exercised all ecclesiastical functions through the instrumentality of its own Brethren, so did it remain supreme in its own lands, where it actually maintained the right of visitation in the episcopal third of the Ordensland. Nay more, save in Ermeland, all the bishops and canons were Brethren of the Order. These facts explain the unbroken unity of the Order's State, and the fidelity of the clergy to the Teutonic Knights even when these were engaged in a dispute with Rome. For such disputes inevitably arose as soon as the Knights, having made themselves thoroughly at home in Prussia, began to climb the steep paths of secular statecraft. Thereupon the favour of the Curia was withdrawn. The Roman See promptly began to regard with that light-hearted aloofness upon which Rome's supremacy over all temporal powers depended, the spiritual brotherhood which had blossomed into a secular landlord. Thenceforward the Order's State, like every other State, was no more than a tool to be handled in the changeful combinations of ecclesiastical policy.

It is true that the Order's unprecedented freedom from the restrictions imposed by Church government necessarily inhibited the straightforward development of its State; for where Church and State were almost identical, improvement of the State became inconceivable without a complete transformation of religious life. For the time being, however, the effective unification of State authority and the vigorous advance of German immigration completed the speedy Germanization of the country. What ensued was not a simple dilution of the Prussians with Germans, but a transformation of the aboriginals. Amid the encircling abundance of German life, the last vestiges of the Old Prussian language and Prussian manners and customs were effaced. By the opening of the fourteenth century the language of the conquerors had become practically universal, the Germans having been forbidden to talk Prussian to their servants. Fifty years later when, at court festivities in Marienburg, a Prussian singer appeared among the German musicians, the laughing knights presented him with a hundred rotten walnuts for, they said, "no-one had been able to understand the poor Prussian." As late as the sixteenth century in some churches interpreters had to translate German sermons to the congregation, while in ultra-secret nocturnal meetings a heathen priest would here and there sacrifice a ram in honour of the old gods. Two hundred years later Matthäus Prätorius came across scattered fishermen who were hostile to the Church, clung to an ancient faith in non-Christian miracles, and were regarded by him as "genuine Old-Prussian pagans." But soon after Luther's time the last vestiges of the original Prussian speech began to die out. Only the tenacious Lithuanian inhabitants of Shalauen and Nadrauen continue to preserve their ancient ways, still speaking their melodious speech and singing their old folk-songs, while the men wear bast shoes, and the girls don as head-covering the richly adorned blue kasavaika.

Thus was the valley of the Vistula brought into the general movement of history, and thus was the New Germany founded—a land which, though in political and military union with the rest of Germany, was strongly averse to conquests beside the Gulf of Riga into which the Western Dvina pours its waters. Let us briefly summarize the characteristics of the colonization of Old Prussia and of what are now the Baltic provinces of Russia, respectively, for they alone explain the wide difference between their subsequent history. Prussia was Germanized, but in Courland, Livonia, and Estonia, there was no more than a thin stratum of German elements superimposed upon the masses of aboriginal inhabitants. By sea the Germans arrived in small numbers, to find a mixed population of Lithuanians and Finns, who paid rent to the princes of Polotsk. The immigrants took the place of these foreign magnates, assigning the land to the Order, the Church, a few crusaders, and the patriciates of the scanty towns. Thus from the first this implantation had a one-sided aristocratic nature. There was but little trace of a German peasantry, and less and less the farther east one went. A burgher life properly so-called developed only in Riga, Dorpat, and Reval; the other towns retained a purely rural character, being quiet places; and in the whole of Courland there was not a single city of outstanding importance.

The west was more favourably situated in another notable respect. Old Prussia was colonized by Germany at large. Its towns were settlements of easterners, and therefore (as throughout the regions strongly influenced by the Hanseatic League) the municipal books were kept and business letters were written in Low German, the silver currency of Northern Europe was in circulation, trade was sedulously

restricted to the northern regions which had been
occupied by the Low Germans, and the whole trend
of civic life was both bolder and rougher than in High
German towns, which imported, not only the costly
wares of Mediterranean countries, but also the sciences
and arts of the south—a taste for pictures and orna-
mental fountains being brought over the Alps. Such
peasant settlers as there were likewise came chiefly
from the north, finding in Prussia the marshes and dikes
of their homeland. But in the ruling class, that of the
Order, High Germans predominated, for their
immigration took place by land, and the South German
knights were loath to prolong their journey farther
eastward, finding sufficient warlike occupation in
Prussia. That was why the official language of the
Teutonic Knights in Prussia was a Middle German
which everyone could understand. Livonia, on the
other hand, was mainly settled from North Germany,
and the Letts still speak of their German conquerors
as "Saxons." The Low Germans who came thither
(chiefly Westphalians) arrived on the Hanse trading
ships, above all by way of Lübeck. In the fifteenth
century entrance into the Livonian branch of the
Order was reserved to the North Germans, and after
that the higher posts among the Teutonic Knights
were almost always filled by members of the West-
phalian families of Plettenberg, Kettler, and Mallin-

krodt. Low German prevailed throughout the country until Luther's Bible gained a footing for High German here also. As late as the close of the sixteenth century Balthasar Rüssow of Reval wrote his chronicle in Low German. A fourth far-reaching difference was super-added. Whereas in Prussia the Order took its stand upon a quasi-modern territorial authority, the eastern territories were disintegrated by medieval anarchy. The provisus of the Order, the archbishop of Riga, claimed jurisdiction over the German magnates, some-times even calling in the Lithuanian heathens to aid him, and he protected the maltreated Letts against the Germans. No less insubordinate were the three great towns. Sanguinary battles often raged round the walls of Wittensteen, a fortress the knights had built to keep Riga in subjection. Subsequently the vassals in the country districts began to have a pride of their own. The archbishop and the Order, the canonical nobility and the nobility of the Brotherhood, the burghers and the knights, weakened themselves by struggles for precedence.

Thus did our people, upon this narrow stage, fore-stall those two main trends of colonial policy which were subsequently to guide Britain and Spain with equal success upon the vast expanses of America. In the unhappy clash between races inspired by fierce mutual enmity, the blood-stained savagery of a quick war of annihilation is more humane, less revolting, than the specious clemency of sloth, which keeps the vanquished in the state of brute beasts while either hardening the hearts of the victors or reducing them to the dull brutality of those they subjugate. An amalgamation of the invaders with the primitive inhabitants was impossible in Old Prussia, where neither the climate of the country nor the culture of those who dwelt in it was attractive to the Germans, and the incapacity of the autochthons for a national State life (even under Slav auspices) was obvious. Thus when, by a kindly gift, the master bestowed his own language on the servant, he smoothed the latter's path to a higher civilization. At a much lower level than the Prussians stood the Letts and the sombre Finnish Estonians, who formed nothing better than petty States with very little community life, dwelling in the monotonous wastes of their prairies, bogs, and pine-forests, unacquainted with the luxuriance of oaks or the liveliness of royal deer-hunts—still possible in the less severe clime of Prussia. In the then anarchical condition of these north-eastern wilds, and owing to the small number of the German immigrants, it was impossible to give such tribes averse to culture the boon of the German language and German civilization. The conquerors kept the vanquished out of touch with German manners and customs, being content

that the Estonians should faithfully do their toilsome
duty as serfs. The non-German to whom the German
lord of the manor assigned a plot of land with the
obligations of socage attached, was no better than a
bondslave. The landlords took joint measures for the
capture of runaways, and thus made the escape of those
whom they maltreated practically impossible. The
result was the formation in these north-eastern marches
of a populace without rights, for it consisted of
underlings who were substantially slaves, whereas the
Prussian peasants, learning to speak German, simultaneously acquired German freedom. In the larger
towns a few fine educational institutions were gradually
established, such as (about 1300) the excellent cathedral
grammar school of Reval; but those who were not given
the chance of learning German were denied such
educational facilities. "Among a thousand peasants,"
complains Balthasar Rüssow, "you will hardly find
one able to say the Lord's Prayer." Children began
yelling from fear, and dogs slunk out of the way,
when a German entered the smoke-begrimed hut of
an Estonian. During the fine nights of their short, hot
summer, the oppressed natives would sit under a birch
(the tree most commonly mentioned in their tedious
verses) and furtively intone a hymn of hatred for the
German sheep-stealers: "Puff yourselves up, you
Germans, thinking yourselves better than anyone else

in the world; you dislike all that we poor Estonians do; may you be plunged, therefore, into the depths of hell." This hatred continued to animate the serfs for centuries, being countered by the harshness of the masters, until at length, in the days of the Russian dominion, the German nobles decided to liberate their peasants from bondage to the glebe. By this contrast we can measure all that Old Prussia gained through being Germanized.

Hardly had the subjugation of Prussia been completed, than the Order began to extend its plans to the country westward of the Vistula, to Pomerellen, then in the hands of Polish vassals. This step was determined, not only by the restless nature of a militarist State, but also by a serious political need. As the land passed increasingly under cultivation, the Vistula ceased to be a natural frontier, and the young colony could not maintain itself in default of direct communication with the strong root of its power—with Germany. It would certainly have been better for Germany if the Order had been ready to continue its work of Germanization hand in hand with Brandenburg, the other north-eastern march of the realm. But so remote a horizon was beyond the political scope of a medieval territory. Already, it is true, the fates of these two marches, which naturally had much in common, were becoming intertwined; but only to this extent that, turn and turn about, they were involved in conflicts with the peoples of the east. As soon as the power of the Ascaniers in Brandenburg collapsed, the Teutonic Knights valiantly took up their position to defend the breach in German civilization, and once more after the victory of the Poles in Prussia the House of Hohenzollern took measures to restore order in distracted Brandenburg. But to begin with there was open hostility between the Ascaniers and the German seigniors. For a long time, with the diplomatic finesse which has always characterized aristocrats, the Order had by peaceful means been acquiring strips of land in Pomerellen. Like Rome it knew how to take advantage of men's spiritual needs as a lever to increase its temporal power. Many an anxious Christian found it possible to secure mental tranquillity by giving considerable sums of money to the German overlords. When Valdemar, King of Denmark, had to relinquish the crusade he had vowed to undertake in the Holy Land, he atoned his fault by making a large gift to the Teutonic Knights. Elsewhere the economic superiority of the Germans favoured the position of the Order amid the heedless frivolity of the Slavs. Its excellent administration, which was conducted in accordance with the principles of oriental finance (advantageously applied by Venice and Naples as well), provided it with ample quantities of ready cash, which gave tremendous power in days when payments were mostly made in kind. Sometimes the Knights would ransom a Wendish prince who had been made prisoner of war, or they would pay the debts of one of the Wedells, or give a valuable charger to one of the Bonins—reaping in return territorial accessions. At length arrived the welcome hour when they could form a stately province out of these scattered estates to the west of the Vistula.

When the line of the dukes of Pomerellen became extinct, the Poles contested the indisputable right of the margraves of Brandenburg to the orphaned duchy. King Wladislaus of Poland appealed to the Order for help in expelling the Ascaniers from Danzig. The Knights had recourse to their bold and well-tried devices, driving out the Brandenburgers, but also the Poles, and they demanded an exorbitant reward for this work of liberation. When the Poles refused to pay, the Order bought from the Brandenburgers their claims to Pomerellen (1311), thrust out everyone who supported Poland, organized the duchy between the Vistula and the Leba as part of the Ordensland, and conciliated the peasants by mitigating the harshness of the serfdom that had been maintained by the Slavs. Thus were added to the towns that had long been flourishing four new and important ones: Kulm, which had in former days been the capital of the region;

the strongly fortified Elbing; the lovely Thorn; and the wealthy Danzig. This last which was an old-established Slav and Danish settlement, enriched by only a few Germans during the last hundred years, flourished abundantly under the rule of the Knights. A fortress was built by the Order to replace the Slav ducal palace, and beside the Altstadt (Old Town) and the Slav fishermen's quarters, the Hakelwerk rapidly outvying both, there sprang up the German Jungstadt (New Town) of Danzig, whose growth was greatly promoted by the new sovereign lords.

This bold acquisition necessarily led to an outburst of the Polish hatred which so much had already been done to provoke. At this juncture the Teutonic Knights were being troubled in the east by the onslaughts of a more formidable enemy, the savage Lithuanians, then at the climax of their power, ruling a dominion that extended as far as Kiev and Vladimir. A perturbed frontier existence was the lot of the Germans eastward of Königsberg. Watchmen of the Order, maintained out of the heavy "Wartgeld" exacted from the region, dwelt in the little fortresses and blockhouses of the wide wilderness that stretched along the border. Thus was the Ordensland safeguarded against the barbarians. Several times a year the warning signals of the frontier guards would be sounded. When this happened, women and children would seek the refuges provided by the Order, and the militia would be called up. Mounting their little ponies and shouting as they rode, the enemy laid waste the countryside with fire and sword, and carried off into servitude all persons they took alive, having great need of bondslaves to till their depopulated land. Such has been the unchanging method of warfare among the barbarians of the east, and it was still employed by Peter the Great against the Germans. Indeed, their enmity was only to be expected. How could the heathen look kindly on neighbours whose religion made war against the unconverted a holy task? Still less could the Order fail to be militant so long as the Lithuanian province of Samaiten thrust itself like a wedge between East Prussia and Courland, and even severed the German coastal strip in twain.

The Teutonic Knights were thus surrounded by foes when, at the opening of the fourteenth century, a new enemy approached. These religious Orders were forsaken in an epoch when the monarchial system was ripening in Europe. As a satrap of the new monarchy in France, Pope Clement V, at Avignon, undertook the destruction of the Templars. The Hospitallers, menaced by a similar onslaught, sedulously enhanced their power by the conquest of Rhodes. Now, having received a complaint from the insubordinate archbishop of Riga, the Pope fulminated against the German

Brotherhood, placing it under the ban, and declaring: "The thorns of vice shall be eradicated from the vineyard of the Lord."

A statesmanlike notion saved the Order from this peril. Undertaking a step which had long been hindered by the jealousy of the Knights, it removed to Prussia the Grand Mastership, which was the centre of gravity of its power. A hundred years after the foundation of the body, Acre, the centre of its structure and the last stronghold of the Latins in the East, had fallen into the hands of the Egyptians (1291). The main cause of this disaster was the insubordination of the Templars and the Hospitallers. After that, the Grand Masters, hoping to inaugurate a new crusade, had held their court at Venice. But how could one and the same town be expected to shelter in permanence the chiefs of two mutually mistrustful and ambitious aristocracies? Of the seven pillars which, according to the ancient manual of the Order, supported the Hospital of St. Mary, three—Armenia, Apulia, and Rumania—had fallen, or were on the verge of falling. In Alemannia and Austria the Order was a wealthy landowner, providing a warm corner for the younger sons of the aristocracy; and the popular wit was wont to make mock of the tedious ceremonies that went on at the Grand Master's court. "Undress, dress once more; eat, drink, sleep, and snore; German lords work full sore," ran the ditty. The Landmaster of Livonia at length shared his authority with the Church. In Old Prussia alone had the Order unlimited powers of State. There, then, at Marienburg, should be the new focus of the Grand Master's rule. It was a happily chosen capital, keeping oversight from the west upon the still unsecured Pomerellen, in close touch with Germany and the Baltic, approximately equidistant from Thorn and Königsberg. When Grand Master Siegfried von Feuchtwangen entered Marienburg (1309), and took into his own hands the office of Landmaster of Prussia, it had been decided that the Order was to turn its back upon the outworn romanticism of a crusade into the Holy Land and seriously devote itself to the far more promising task of statecraft.

Very soon, indeed, it became plain how lasting a strength would accrue to the Order thanks to its temporal power. Maintaining at the papal court a permanent representative, the procurator of the Order, the Grand Master was kept thoroughly well-informed about the wishes and intentions of the Curia, was aware that where Rome pastured her sheep she expected a good deal of wool, so he had recourse to the time-honoured method of using palm-oil. Then, after a while, he made his way to Avignon, and speedily learned that the State of the German seigniors was in

a safer position than were the Templars, who had
no State. When subsequently the Order, in accordance
with its aggressive policy, claimed over the Polish
bishops in Pomerellen the rights it already exercised
in Prussia, going so far as to forbid the payment of
Peter's Pence, the Prussian people was by that time
inspired with the rationalism of colonials, and had
absorbed the defiant spirit of its German masters. The
estates of Kulmerland withheld Peter's Pence, and,
being put under an interdict, "did not for that reason
find their bread and beer any less tasty than before."
The Order was equally successful in its relations with
Poland. The conditions prevailing in the two States
and the disposition of the two peoples impelled them
to make war on one another. The national sentiment
of Poland was now becoming intense. The crown
prince of Poland was wooing the princess who seemed
likely to become queen of Lithuania, and the eastern
realm into which Old Prussia, colonized by the
Teutonic Knights, had now developed, founded, as
a symbol of its growing importance, the Order of the
White Eagle. There was looming for the first time the
danger (to be averted for a space by the favour of
fortune) of that union between Poland and Lithuania
which was to materialize a century later and seal the
fate of the Teutonic Knights. King Casimir the Great
was personally favourable to the Germans, and

encouraged German immigrants to settle in his towns; but in the long run he was unable to withstand the chauvinism of his nobles, so he forbade the Polish cities to have their law cases settled by appeal in Magdeburg, and established a Polish court in Cracow. Incessantly the Polish aristocrats urged him to declare war against the Ordensland. How could he possibly endure, they asked, that the Germans should steal his last stretch of coast in addition to robbing him of the lower reaches of the Vistula? How could the Polish waywode bear that on land which had been Polish from time immemorial the Order's bailiffs should take away from the starosts the leather scourges with which it had been usual to enforce discipline upon the serfs; that the German landlords should gibe at the Polish nobles as being no better than raw peasants—who, however, knew very well the art of taking off a pretty lady's shoe, filling it with mead, and draining it at a draught? In a word, was it to be permitted that the strict State and the easy-going customs of the Germans should be substituted for the anarchic crudity of Polish Slavs? War ensued, and went on for thirty years, with fluctuating results and frequent interruptions. At the fiercely contested battle of Plowce, the Knights' army was near to destruction when Heinrich von Plauen, bailiff of Pomesanien, managed to save the situation. The peace of Kalisz, in 1343,

registered the complete victory of the Germans.
Poland renounced her claim to Pomerellen and certain
border regions, including a considerable portion of the
famous Kujavien, a wheatland between the Vistula
and the Netze. Throughout the struggle, Rome supported the Poles with her spiritual weapons. All the
closer, therefore, did the Order draw to the Empire,
which in prosperous days it was too much inclined to
forget. Now, under Emperor Louis the Bavarian, the
old quarrel between State and Church was revived
as a war of principles: Ghibelline authors began a
pen campaign against Rome; our electors manfully in-
sisted upon freedom in their choice of an emperor,
irrespective of France, and of the Pope who was a
French tool; and, for the first time within the bosom
of the Church, the Minorites contended that the
Council was superior to the Pope. In this great
struggle the Grand Master openly espoused the cause
of the Emperor, whom he declared to be "his prince,
and the best-loved man in the realm."

Thus the secular statecraft of this religious community had achieved a safe rounding-off of the
Knights' domain. Guided by the same secular political
aims, Grand Master Werner von Orselen decided at
this time (1329) to modify the original statutes of the
modest hospital Brotherhood in accordance with the

bolder outlooks of a Baltic great power—in so far as this was possible while continuing to pay due regard to persistent ecclesiastical conventions. After the victory over Poland, the Lithuanian peril was less ominous. The Order now assumed the offensive against the peoples that lay to the east, with the result that in a few decades it reached the climax of its fame. Orselen was followed in the Grand Master's chair by a number of talented men, such as Luther von Braunschweig (a master of minstrelsy), Dietrich von Altenburg, and, above all, Winrich von Kniprode. This last, a man from the lower Rhine, was a light-hearted and chivalrous knight, but nonetheless a cautious and far-seeing statesman. He was as much in tune with the ideas of his time as anyone should be who is to exert a profound influence on that time; yet he was a cheerful man of the world, more free-spirited than most of his contemporaries. In a word, like Henry of Navarre, he was one of those joyous, splendour-loving, and victorious princely figures to whose name the peoples come to attach the memory of their "good old days." Under Winrich, during the three decades from 1351 to 1382, the State of the Teutonic Knights actually became a great power, being (like Spain a hundred years later) the centre and the training-ground of Latin chivalry.

In sober truth, it was only thanks to the strictness

of a sacred brotherhood and the serious duties imposed by weighty political tasks that the decayed knighthood of the age was able to regain its vanished nobility. In an epoch of ecclesiastical contention, the religious fervour of the early Middle Ages had fled. What had allured knights errant to take the vow of service in the Prussian Crusade was no longer Christian enthusiasm, but only a lust for adventure. It would have been vain to seek even the simple, harsh pugnacity of those who, as was said of the early crusaders to the Holy Land, "lively, bold, and gay, pious night and day," hewed a path through a world of foes. The character-traits of the much extolled "second knighthood," were artificially refined. These men were but epigones, the devotees of the second chivalry, who disclosed themselves in the fourteenth century after the wild interregnum of the empire. The populace was beginning to turn its eyes yearningly towards the past in search of its political ideals, towards the age of the Hohenstaufens, and the poet modestly admits: "Most masters hew their way mightily *before* they reach the forest of art." While in any case the harmony and depth of modern sensibilities makes it hard for us to find congenial the wild leaps, I would even say the desultory negligence, of the mental life of medievals, we are positively horrified by the coldness of heart and poverty of spirit manifested by the second chivalry.

In deliberate imitation of the past, fair ladies were extravagantly bepraised by knights whose shameless behaviour and dissolute lives were in hateful contrast with their ornate phraseology. Although the childish belief in wonders had long vanished, adults still felt their imaginations kindled by old books about the adventures of heroes. Whereas the nobility once fought enthusiastically on behalf of the sublime schemes of imperial statecraft, the German knight of later days wandered hither and thither without plan and without dignity, swaggering as he sought adventures in lands ranging from Hungary to Spanish Morocco. Such fantastic activities were exceptionally unbecoming to the Germans. It is true that even in the better days of genuine chivalry our people tried to learn from the Latins, yet before long they had their own Hohenstaufen emperors and their Walther von der Vogelweide who could unhesitatingly be ranked with the greatest heroes and singers of the Romans. But amid the terrible confusions of the fourteenth and fifteenth centuries, Germany could only produce jejune and prosaic princes who knew how to hold their own against the burgherdom. Unattractive, almost weakly, seems the noble figure of Frederick the Handsome, Duke of Austria, when compared with that of the Black Prince; as against the heroes of the Hundred Years' War, rough and shopkeeper-like appear those members of the Austrian knighthood who wanted to make their king repay them for every shoe their horses cast during a campaign.

Of all the German lands, Prussia alone could at this time rank with the west in respect of the triumphant position of chivalry. For it was no mere pugnacity or love of adventure which impelled the Teutonic Knights into the Lithuanian war. The essential qualities of a militarist State were at work. The more capable among the Grand Masters knew very well how to maintain religious discipline in the Order, how to discourage participation in the tournament craze of the new times, and yet how to turn to chivalry's own advantage its finer imaginative trends. "It was in Prussia that he became a knight"—such was for generations the highest praise that could be given to a Christian nobleman; and the knight errant who had been in Prussia would proudly wear the black cross of the Teutonic Knights to the end of his days. Even kings regarded it as an honour when the Order enrolled them among its associate brethren, and no higher praise could Chaucer find for the knight among his Canterbury pilgrims than to say: "In Lettow had he reysed and in Ruce." It was the ambition during that epoch to vie with the warlike renown of the conquerors of the Holy Sepulchre. The Flemish knight Guillebert de Lannoy, who described "la reyse de Prusse" in

his candid diary, sometimes went so far as to stigmatize
the "mécréans de Lettau" as "Saracens." From all
the countries of Europe, "thanks to God, to the love
of honour, and to the spirit of chivalry," bold young
blades made for Lithuania in the hope of winning there
the golden spurs. In the Christian camp the banner
of the Order would wave from dawn till midday
beneath the walls of an enemy fortress; and if, upon the
herald's summons, no one came forward to contest in
single combat a candidate's claim to the distinction
of knighthood, the Grand Master would give the
aspirant St. George's blessing. But even well-tried
knights would set out for Prussia in order to fight there
in the cause of our fair ones. We find among the
guests of the Teutonic Knights, not only Boucicaut,
the French Quixote of a Quixotic era, but also a cold
calculator in the person of Henry, Earl of Derby, who
subsequently, by complicated intrigues, became king
of England and founded the House of Lancaster. Once
there were two kings simultaneously present at the
Grand Master's court: Louis of Hungary and the
chivalrous John of Bohemia (who lost an eye in the
marshes of Lithuania). When such a distinguished
guest arrived, a campaign against the heathen would
be promptly begun "in honour of the noble visitor
and likewise in that of the Maid of supreme virtue
whom we style the Blessed Virgin." When the need

was pressing, the Grand Master devised an exceptional attraction. A "Table of Honour" was set apart for the chosen from among the knights of the Latin countries. Then in all lands became famous the names of the ten who, after a victory of the Order, would be declared the worthiest champions. In a richly adorned tent they would be entertained like the knights of King Arthur's Round Table at a splendid banquet, to the accompaniment of music discoursed by zithers and fifes. It was obvious that such extemporized campaigns could rarely be serious affairs, seldom carefully planned; ere long, indeed, they degenerated into futile and rugged dalliance. Most of the knightly wars of the Middle Ages were brief and tumultuous, if only because of the difficulty of finding fodder for the horses. The Order's guides led the army across the heathland, with the banner of Ragnit, the frontier fortress, in the vanguard. For a few nights they all camped under the open sky: "In moorland find sufficient lair, like him who hunteth fox and hare." Everything in the enemy's land was destroyed, on the simple rule: "What harms them, does us good." As soon as the Christians felt entitled to plume themselves on a glorious victory, they turned about and sought Prussia once more, bringing with them a few Lithuanians, "in leash, like dogs"—though sometimes the barbarians would lure the victorious knights into marshes or wild moors where they could easily be ambushed amid the huge thorny fences which traversed the country. But wherever they went, the Knights were wont to display an almost ostentatious valiancy and ingenuity, as did Commander Hermann von Oppen when he made a sally through the gates of Schönsee, and thus successfully defended the fortress. In time, however, the behaviour of its guests became a nuisance to the Order. Even worse than the regular armies were the thievish camp-followers (the Latin chroniclers call them by the distinctive name of "latrunculi"), who abounded on both sides.

Yet even in such chance-medleys on the grand scale we easily discern the fundamental characteristic of the Order, its Janus' head, with one of the faces directed towards the lucid realm of modern political ideas, the other looking backward into the perplexing dream-world of the Middle Ages. Though irreconcilable, the opposition between Christianity and Paganism had long since been mitigated.

Already during the Grand Mastership of Winrich von Kniprode the Teutonic Knights for the first time made peace with the heathen, thus violating their own statutes. All the more tenaciously, however, did the Ordensland as a State cling to the political purpose for which it had been making war—the determination to lop off the north-westward extension of Lithuania which thrust between the province of the Dvina and that of the Vistula. In the year 1398 this aim was substantially fulfilled, for Samaiten was ceded to the Order, so that the whole of the southern shore of the Baltic now belonged to the Germans. This was not exclusively achieved by the raids of distinguished guests. On many occasions the entire armed and organized force of the militarist State took the field, as happened in 1370, the most glorious year of the Teutonic Knights' history. It was then that the Chief Marshal of the Order under the great Winrich, the man whose heart was as hard as his name Henning Schindekopf, fell as victor at the terrific battle of Rudau, the memory of which is still vivid in Old Prussia. Success at Rudau had been prepared for by the arms-clubs of the citizens. These confraternities enrolled patricians as well as guildsmen. Circumstances permitting, every spring they marched in proper order out through the gates "to fetch King Lent," as ancient custom prescribed. But when war-conditions prevailed. they assembled round the banner of the Order under the leadership of their commander. Winrich had known how to combine merriment with seriousness in promoting the soldierliness of his burghers, systematically organizing in every town the shooting at the popinjay, and encouraging the excellence of crossbowmen by State prizes. Simultaneously the landlords and the peasants were becoming accustomed to the leadership of their commanders, in accordance with strict rule, themselves in complete armour and mounted on horses that were also mail-clad, or partially so, this varying from place to place. The distinguished foreign guests, too, were under the command of the Teutonic Knights, who were still bearded in compliance with ancient custom and wore long, white cloaks of imposing aspect. All other flags had to be dipped (in this German borderland where the dominant imperial ensign had never yet waved) when the standard of the Order on which the gracious figure of the Virgin was displayed moved onward in advance of the Chief Marshal. Unless the Grand Master himself took command, the orders of the Chief Marshal decided everything. When peace prevailed in this turbulent east, the last-named official usually resided at Königsberg; but when war raged he would be near the front, attended by the general staff. The unyielding decisions of a court martial were imposed on all the refractory—whether guests, Prussians, or German seigniors—and especially on those who interfered with the prescribed march. Even in camp the altar surrounded by flags bore witness to the religious significance of the affair. Thus was the heavy cavalry of the proud nobles trained to co-operate harmoniously with the infantry militiamen. There was a use for light cavalry, the Turcopoles, as well. It was here, too, that the heavy missiles of artillery first came into general service, this arm being speedily adopted by the Knights, who were not backward in turning to account, at the beginning of the fourteenth century, the inventive genius of their warlike towns. The old monastic duty of care for the sick and injured now ministered to the temporal power; and a great alms-house was built at Marienburg for the care of those brethren that had grown infirm. But in the hearts of the Lithuanians and Slavs the old national hatred of the Germans continued to glow. When a stronghold beside the Memel was stormed by the Christians, hundreds of the heathen offered their necks to an elderly priestess, lest any should be taken alive by the Teutons. Here and there, however, we begin to encounter signs of humane feeling on our side. Large numbers of maltreated serfs fled from Lithuania to enjoy the milder rule of the Order, which accepted the refugees, with the proviso that they would be sent back as soon as all Lithuania should accept the Knights' rule.

Whereas in the wars of the Teutonic Knights a strictly monarchical system was enforced, in the matter of political administration an aristocratic spirit of discussion prevailed. "It is well for people to take counsel together"—this saying, confirmed by the example of Jesus whose habit it was to ask the pious advice of the apostles, indicates the ecclesiastico-aristocratic nature of the basic ideas of the Order's constitution. When a Grand Master died, his deputy summoned to Marienburg all the chiefs of the Teutonic Knights, including the Landmasters of Germany and Livonia. When they had assembled, the bells of the castle church pealed to announce that the thirteen would by ballot elect a successor to the vacant post, one who would govern the State of Christ. But though the mightiest kings of Christendom would address the Grand Master as "Our Dear Brother," he could only decide freely and without challenge where trivial and commonplace matters were concerned. The five principal authorities next to himself—the Grand Commander, who would function as deputy when he died; the Chief Marshal, who acted as generalissimo; the Head Almoner, who presided over all the charitable institutions; the Sumptuary or Drapier, who had charge of the wardrobe and the armoury; and the Treasurer—must have their approval asked before every important decision. Nothing that seriously affected the country and its inhabitants could be undertaken without the warrant of both the Grand Master of the Order and the Landmaster of Germany; and several times the last-named, with the support of the other chiefs, deposed a Grand Master who was

exceeding his powers. When the influence of the Order
became widespread, and the Grand Master's relations
with foreign princes grew more intimate, he released
himself by degrees from the petty observances of
monastic discipline, and led a court life marked by
impressive ceremony. But even then the head of the
Baltic State, when he took his meals in the refectory,
was allotted four helpings of each course that he might
have an ample surplus for the poor and for penitents.
Only in cases of the utmost urgency could the Grand
Master take action quite independently and issue a
decree that must be unconditionally obeyed. Of course
even such restricted authority could be most effective
when it was wisely used, this being assured during the
best days of the Order by the almost invariable
election of Grand Masters who were men of outstanding
ability. Just like the position of the Grand Master
in relation to the Teutonic Knights as a whole was
that of the commander of every important fortress,
who was "rather servant than master" of the twelve
brethren who (following the precedent of the twelve
apostles) formed his council.

The only thing that held this aristocracy together
was the terrible severity of the Brotherhood's discipline.
The "Rules, Laws, and Customs" of the Order can
still show us to-day to what a pitch was developed the
art of dominating the Knights and making them

useful. A candidate for admission to the body must be capable of complete self-renunciation. In this spirit he took the vow of poverty, chastity, and obedience, "which are the essential foundations of a spiritual life." Having been sworn, he was given a sword, a piece of bread, and an old habit. He was forbidden to use his family coat-of-arms, to associate with the secular, to live in luxurious towns, to ride out alone, to read or write letters. Sleeping partially dressed, and with his sword ready to hand, a brother was summoned by bells every night at the Canonical Hours, and four times to the prayers of the daily office; and every Friday he must submit himself to monastic mortification. If his superiors appointed him to any post, no matter whether at Riga or Venice, he had no option but to obey; and when September 14th, the day on which the discovery of the true cross was commemorated, came round, he must resign his functions to the Chapter of his province. His record was kept in the archives. Should a brother fall into sin, a secret Chapter would be held upon his case, opening with a mass and ending with prayer. The offender might be degraded to the servants' table, or might actually be chastized, "the blows being appropriate to the magnitude of the wrongdoing." But the Grand Master might be clement, for if in one hand he held the rod of punishment, in the other

was the staff of mercy. Only in the case of "the two
most grievous offences"—desertion of the colours and
intercourse with the heathen, was no atonement
possible. The sinner was deprived of his cross, and was
permanently expelled from the Order. Requital was
exacted beyond the grave. If among the possessions of
a deceased Teutonic Knight more was found than the
pitiful amount permitted by the statutes, his body was
buried in unconsecrated ground. The numerous non-
knighted brethren of the Order were subjected to the
same monastic discipline. These wore the black cross
upon a grey cloak, and were given various duties, but
most of them were light cavalrymen. The Grand
Master was also surrounded by many lay servants and
courtiers, who became more numerous as the power
of the State grew; they were Prussian aristocrats who
could do political service to the Order; also men of
learning, artists, retainers, and subalterns. It was
under stress of this formidable discipline, in a world
that showed itself great and splendid to the Order,
but harsh and petty to individuals, that Grand Master
Conrad von Jungingen, on his deathbed, adjured those
who would elect his successor not to choose his brother.
Indeed, a near future was to show that when all the
less exalted impulses were thus inhumanly suppressed,
neither freedom of the spirit nor a steady political
advance was to be anticipated.

The law-code continued to speak of "the gold of love, which makes the poor who have it rich, and the rich who lack it poor." A few great hospitals under the supervision of the Head Almoner, and the well-provided almshouse at Marienburg for the shelter of infirm knights, still bore witness to the days when the Order, which now occupied three princely thrones, had been wont, in the tents of Acre, to care for the wounded; and even now every tenth loaf was at the disposal of the poor. But more and ever more did the political and military aims of the Teutonic Knights thrust themselves into the foreground. It often seemed as if the religious nature of their corporation was nothing more than a means whereby could be enforced that silent military subjection which in days when uncontrolled personal ambition had become supreme could only be maintained by the dread gravity of religious vows. When at the refectory table where silence prevailed during meals, this silence was broken by a reading from the Bible, the Lesson to be chosen by the Priest-Brother would usually be one about "the knights of the days of Joshua or Moses." Again and again the younger brethren would be emphatically reminded of the exhortation in I Maccabees, 2, 50: "And now, my children, be zealous for the law, and give your lives for the covenant of your fathers." It was an endless outpost-duty. By day and by night the horses of the messengers were ready saddled in the stables, that the commands of the Grand Master, or his information regarding the death of a brother, could at a moment's notice be conveyed from fortress to fortress—arrangements being made for this posting-service throughout Central and Southern Europe. Any day an inspector of the Order might arrive to demand keys and accounts from a stronghold, and all the brethren were charged to acquaint him with any breach of the rules that applied simultaneously to every keep in the wide realm.

With the enforcement of such pitiless supervision, the finances of the Order could not but thrive. According to a poet, the pennies could say that at Marienburg they were quite at home—the place was theirs. Down to the fifteenth century in the accounts of Königsberg, which are still preserved in the archives of the city, we can detect no trace of peculation. Among the Teutonic Knights a thoroughly modern idea, that of scientific book-keeping, had already been realized. The State budget was quite distinct from the pocket-money of the prince, whose privy purse was replenished from the revenues of specified landed estates. It was natural that prosperity and culture should abound beyond compare when the capital and the skilled labour of a well-conducted but youthful nation joined forces with the elaborate notions of Papal, Oriental, and Hanseatic statecraft, and all combined could exert their fertilizing powers upon the luxuriance of a virgin soil. Where the nobles themselves ruled under the guidance of a sacred law, there could be no trouble from one of the greatest curses of the Middle Ages—breaches of the public peace by the minor members of a predatory nobility. This was not the place for the landed gentry to sing, as they sang in the Empire: "Let's rob and reive—for who can blame what the best men do with no thought of shame?" The landed gentry and their squires, though well established in the west and in the highlands, could not at first venture to defy the mighty Order. They were in the good graces of the great Winrich, who formed out of these land-lords the core of his mounted militia. They were subject to the jurisdiction of the Order, and the brisk grain trade made it desirable for them to keep on the best possible terms with the towns. The rest of the free population of the countryside became gradually fused into a compact mass, and the larger bulk of the freemen of Old Prussia had chartered rights. Even the forced labour that had been exacted from those bound to the soil was mitigated because the Teutonic Knights, recognizing the importance of the rapidly developing monetary economy, were glad to allow the corvée of the serfs to be transformed into the payment of rent. The principle adopted from the

Hanse burghers of abolishing restrictions upon change
of domicile, was favourable to agriculture and promoted liberty, though the peasant's desire that his
farm should be kept in the family hindered an excessive
to and fro movement of the population. Besides, how
could the countryman be permanently kept in an
oppressed condition when the unceasing struggle with
the encroachments of the sea and the freshets of the
streams made continual demands upon the personal
efforts of the peasants? The aristocracy of the German
seigniors in Old Prussia grew more and more inclined
—as the power of the patriciates in the towns and the
junkers in the country tended to increase—to heed the
poet's warning to the monarch of the Middle Ages:
"To thee the poor man looks for aid." Folk-singers
gave the highest possible praise to the great Winrich
by declaring him to have been the peasant's friend.

The Church remained dependent. The monasteries,
more especially, were closely supervised by the Order,
and mendicant friars could not solicit alms from the
pious unless they had secured a licence. Only in
Ermeland, where the Order had not succeeded in
placing its own nominees in the cathedral chapter,
did there early begin unfortunate disputes between
the bishopric and the Teutonic Knights. Still, this
rare exception does not invalidate the praiseworthy
fact that the Order's domain was the most extensive

one in medieval Germany where a unified system of law prevailed. Every commander of a fortress in the Ordensland was also prefect of the territorial administration, and president of the landthing or provincial assembly. Even the most powerful towns had to respect his authority. The Grand Master had regulated the rights of the towns by a general form of charter, which could not be modified without his consent. He alone decided about the freedom of trade and the admission of foreigners, and specified the season for navigation on the Vistula. To him the country owed a uniform system of weights and measures; and coins could only be issued from his mint at Thorn.

Yet the position of the great towns of the Ordensland, which early joined the Hanseatic League—a German concern—was, according to modern political conceptions, no less incomprehensible than was the relation of the other Hanse towns to their respective territorial authorities. The Hanse towns "which were under two masters" (in Prussia they were six in number: Danzig, Elbing, Thorn, Kulm, Königsberg, and little Braunsberg—for the wealthy Memel stood aloof from the League) in their general Hanseatic diets, or in the diets of the Prussian Hanse towns held at Marienburg or Danzig, would decide to make war on kings with whom the Order was at peace. In negotiations between the Teutonic Knights and Lithuania, they would mediate, playing the part of a neutral State; or they would request the Grand Master to intervene with the queen of Denmark upon a purely Hanseatic matter. Harsh necessity, the serious demands of political work, and the unacknowledged but certainly extant recognition that the splendour of its dominion had a very insecure foundation—compelled the Order to make light of its knightly prejudices, to moderate its lust for power, and to behave as a faithful ally of the towns of Low Germany. The League and the Order were akin as German aristocracies amid semi-barbarian peoples, as self-satisfied conquerors of regions where alien tongues were spoken. The League could only maintain its footing in foreign parts by means of severe and almost monastic discipline in its factories. Like the life of religious brotherhoods, the merchant's trade was wrapped in profound mystery. The "Osterlings" (the eastern cities of Danzig, Elbing, Thorn, etc.) contemplated wider horizons than did the inland towns of Germany; they alone, among our urban communities, carried on a far-sighted policy towards the Order; and they were at one with the Teutonic Knights in the endeavour to ensure that the trade routes between the interior and the seaports should be kept open and secure. An alliance was so natural that the growth of the two powers was simultaneous, and both were doomed to speedy decay when an irreparable breach between them occurred. The most glorious year of the Order was reached in 1370, and the same date marks the climax of Hanse power. When Grand Master Winrich received news of the terrible slaughter of commanders and knights by the Lithuanians at Rudau, Waldemar Atterdag, the Dane, was living at his court as a suitor, having come to implore the Order's aid because the burgher power of the seventy-seven Hanse towns had enforced a right of veto upon the Danish succession. He had been compelled to sign the peace treaty of Stralsund, in which he promised that thenceforward no one should ascend the throne of Denmark without the approval of the Hanseatic League. A few decades later three Prussian towns stood sponsor for the royal word of Albert of Sweden.

Although none of the cities of the Ordensland could give the lie to the German couplet, "Lübeck, incomparable town, of wealth and beauty wears the crown," still of all the "Osterlings" Danzig came nearest to vying with the famous port ten miles from the mouth of the Trave. A dangerous element in the young State, indeed, was Danzig, an unduly powerful community, with its proud patriciate, its enthusiastic guildsmen, and its Polish quarter of Vistula shipmen who are still reputed wild. Danzig was heir to that command of the trade in the eastern Baltic which had in former days been held by Visby on the Swedish island of Gottland. The city was still no less insistent than the Order itself upon the supremacy of Germanic descent and German civilization, and no one who was not of pure Teutonic blood was granted entry into the guilds. Juridical and administrative matters were kept severely apart, in a thoroughly modern way, the former being in the hands of the justiciar and his sheriffs, the latter in those of the burgomaster and his council. The constitution was aristocratic, but on important occasions the assent of the guildsmen was required. More than once the froward guildsmen, riotously emerging from the Guild garden, had made violent demonstrations in front of the patriciate's House of the Round Table; and in this exalted building there had recently been discussion of an audacious plan for wresting the city from the strict tutelage of the Order. For although the Teutonic Knights had established a harmonious commercial system and had never exacted tolls on home commerce, they demanded poundage upon imports. Indeed the Ordensland had now become a purchaser on the large scale, and thus aroused the monopolist envy of the Hanseatic League; with the aid of a papal dispensation, it was carrying on trade of its own, especially in amber, which no one except a servant of the Order was allowed to collect in its territory. It often claimed a preferential right of purchase where the goods imported by its towns were concerned; was not restricted in respect of its own activities by the vetos on export which it sometimes decreed; and had become so vigorous a corn-chandler that no less than six thousand loads of rye were once stored in seven of its fortresses. It had factors at Bruges, in the towns of Prussia, and at Lemberg which was the centre of Polish trade.

The Order's Baltic policy only becomes comprehensible in the light of its relations with the Hanseatic League. Estonia, whose knights had long ago entered into an alliance with the German Brotherhood, was in 1346 completely won over to the Ordensland when the Landmaster of Livonia gave the King of Denmark aid in suppressing a dangerous revolt of the Estonian peasants; and then, in pursuit of its well-tried religious policy, proceeded to demand an exorbitant quid pro quo. Thus it came to pass that all the coast between Lake Peipus and the Leba was placed at the disposal of the Teutonic Knights, who promptly began to maintain the peace of the high seas, building themselves a navy for the protection of ordinary maritime commerce. For a good while, now, German merchants had been wont to trust their cogs only in strong fleets upon the unpatrolled waters. At length in the desolating wars that raged in the days of the Union of Kalmar the contentious powers of the north encouraged the

time-honoured practice of piracy by issuing letters of
marque. Thereupon the piratic league of the
Victualling Brothers, led by the aristocratic adventurers Sture and Manteuffel, being dominant in the
Baltic, seized Gottland and converted the venerable
but decayed Visby into a thoroughly fortified robbers'
nest; and its cruisers lurked in every cranny of this
inland sea where bays abound. But what the Scandi-
navian crowns shrank from attempting was boldly
undertaken by the Order in 1398. With its young
navy, backed by the fighting ships of its towns, in its
turn it conquered Gottland, inflicted terrible punishment on the marauders, and patrolled the waters
with ships commissioned to put an end to plunder
on the high seas. Soon the Danes, justifying themselves on the ground of old suzerain rights, established
themselves on the island, but the Order equipped a
new war-fleet, landed an army of 15,000 men in
Gottland, captured two hundred Danish ships, and in
1404 the crusaders' banner waved once more above
the walls of Visby.

The threads of the Order's policy likewise extended
far into the hinterland. So long as the shores of the
Baltic had not yet become objects of Russian ambition,
the Teutonic Knights were often in alliance with the
white tsar as a long-standing foe of the Lithuanians;
but the Grand Master was also careful to send

ambassadors to the rulers of Kazan and Astrakhan, regarding them as a valuable support against the Muscovites. To the Poles and Lithuanians the Order applied the Roman maxim "divide and conquer"; it fanned the flames of the feud between the grand-princely house and Lithuania; and its fortresses gave welcome to all the malcontents in the neighbouring countries. At the beginning of the fourteenth century Duke Vladyslav von Oppeln, an expelled member of the Piasten dynasty, laid before the Teutonic Knights a scheme for the partition of Poland, which thence-forward was to remain upon the chessboard of European policy. But the statecraft of the Order con-tinually returned from such far-reaching designs to simpler tasks. The tie with Germany remained uncer-tain while the Wendish princes of Pomerania were in a position to cut it whenever the fancy took them. The acquisition of Stolpe and Bütow and other strips of land along the border was no safeguard. But at length the danger was averted by securing a trust-worthy road into the Empire, for in 1402, when the Lützelburgers in the Mark were short of money, the Knights were able to take advantage of this by the purchase of Neumark. The burghers and the peasants of the newly acquired territory had no objection to the rule of the German aristocrats; but the previously independent nobles of Neumark were greatly averse to it, for the rural peace that prevailed in the Ordensland did not suit them at all. But the new road into the Empire was of the utmost moment to the economic life of the Order no less than to its political designs, for its German possessions had by now become most extensive, including two commanderies of inexhaustible wealth— Austria and Coblenz.

When we learn that the peoples who lay to the eastward of the Ordensland trembled at the thought of being attacked by its militia, we must not forget that the Teutonic Knights were obeyed by a peasantry that was war-proof, having been steeled in countless fights. During the earlier days of Old Prussia fine villages and luxuriant forests had once flourished where their sites now lay beneath the waters of the Frisches Haff. Even under the rule of the Order the shape of the coast was modified by inroads of the sea. The former entry into the Frisches Haff, the Withlandsort Deep, was silted up just after a fortress had been built to guard it. The sea broke through a new inlet, and the Knights put the peasants to forced labour upon the strong dikes near Rosenberg. Still more arduous was the struggle with the vagaries of the Vistula. A seemingly impenetrable thicket grew above the reeds on the wide marshes between the backwaters of the Vistula and Nogat, until, every spring, came the terror of the country—the freshets that followed the break-up of the ice. Foot-messengers announced the approach of the enemy, which was all the more alarming because it was so slow, but at length the extensive forests were submerged. Even though modern criticism has ruthlessly dispelled the renown of Landmaster Meinhart von Querfurt, we must not therefore regard as wholly fabulous the merits of the Knight with the Waterwheel who is conspicuous among the monuments that adorn the bridge at Dirschau (Tczew). But it was the Order, and not the strength of one man alone, that, by directing the labour of several generations, tamed the mighty river. A chain of dikes was built across the land, and they were safeguarded by a strict dike-law, which was enforced by peasant officials still known as dikegraves and sworn-inspectors. Thus reclaimed and protected, the eyots on the lower reaches of the Vistula were transformed by Dutch colonists into a rich cornland of the north, so that people began to speak of the presumptuous opulence of the local peasants.

In other places, too, agriculture flourished. Sheep-farming was promoted hand-in-glove with the cloth-trade of Thorn, while the falconers of Prussia provided the sportsmen of all countries with the hunting birds that were needed. The bee-keepers of the Masurian forests sent the wax from their hives to the clergy at great distances, and the ordinary wine of Old Prussia was found palatable enough by the uncorrupted taste

of our forbears. Still more important was the timber-
trade. Representatives of the wood merchants in
Danzig and Riga sought their wares in the forests of
Poland, Lithuania, and Volhynia. The tree-trunks,
fastened together in huge rafts, were floated down the
Vistula and the Dvina, sometimes interfering with
other traffic on the rivers—unless St. Barbara had paid
due heed to the prayers of the Vistula shipmen in the
mountain chapel at Sartowitz. Flax took the same
route, to be sampled and docketed by the brokers at
the port of shipment. The overland trade with Poland
and other adjoining countries was a Prussian monopoly;
and as soon as the Order had cut a canal to connect the
Pregel with the Kurisches Haff, the Memel offered a
route for trade with the heart of Lithuania. There the
brisk city of Danzig established a Hanse purchasing
centre at Kovno. This monopoly of inland trade did
not prevent the Grand Master's towns from following
the example of the other Hanse cities; they took part in
the affairs of the international market at Bruges, and
sent their ships into the Bay of Biscay to buy salt at
the mouth of the Loire. But all the chief eastern cities,
the "Osterlings," owed the prosperity of their guildsmen mainly to the extensive trade that was carried on
with the land lying to the north and the east, which
could not do without the products of German agriculture and industry. Fishery on the large scale, a

natural privilege of the masters of the sea, was kept almost entirely in their own hands by the members of the Hanseatic League. Throughout the summer the Hanse fish-curers occupied their huts at Falsterbo in Scania on the south-west point of Sweden, to deal with the herrings as the boats came in with their haul; and thanks to the favour of the harassed Waldemar Atterdag, Danzig was able to establish its fish-depôt there beside that of its rival Lübeck.

Credit was furthered by the law to regulate bank-ruptcy which the Ordensland had inaugurated, and by a well-devised system of bills of exchange. Above all, the overlord saw to it that there should be no barrier to honest trade. Every Commander made sure that under his jurisdiction there should be no hindrance to traffic on the highways. The Order had made the princes of Stettin pledge themselves to extradite all criminals; and from the dukes of Oppeln it exacted the privilege of arresting its own malefactors upon Silesian soil. By commercial treaties the Teutonic Knights had done their utmost to counteract the evil principle of medieval trade, in accordance with which every merchant who suffered wrongful loss was expected to exact compensation from his own co-nationals. For instance, there was such a treaty with England, which already had a consul in Danzig.

Education and culture did not keep pace with this

mighty advance in material well-being. A philistine trend was, throughout the Middle Ages, characteristic of the North Germans, both in the Hanseatic League and among the Teutonic Knights. The seignior vowed to a quasi-monastic life might seek relief from the terrible monotony of the garrison in knightly amusements (though formal jousting was forbidden), in hunting bears, wolves, or lynxes, "not as a mere casual pastime, but as a regular occupation." When the Grand Master held his court, and when princely guests had to be entertained, there would be tournaments, which the Knights could watch though they themselves might not splinter lances; and banquets where, instead of beer, one could drink wine of Chios, Tuscany, or Istria. At Easter the wenches of Marienburg would come to the palace bringing birch-twigs to greet the prince after the Prussian manner, and expecting a suitable gift in return. In the Grand Master's foreign garden and beside his fishpond, many a pleasant hour could be spent, when bustle and display to honour distinguished visitors had become usual at the capital of the Ordensland. But "high-brow" intellectual and artistic luxury seemed inappropriate to the leaders of the rugged militarist State. As late as the fifteenth century one of the Grand Masters was "neither doctor nor clerk," that is to say he could neither read nor write. When Winrich ordered that in every Chapter there should be at least two learned brethren, one theologian and one jurist, his aim certainly was nothing more than the furtherance of the Order's religious and political aims. The law school he founded at Marienburg soon came to naught; and the University of Kulm he planned to establish never materialized. Learned knights were allowed to continue their studies, but the unlearned were not enjoined to learn. Enough if they knew the Lord's Prayer and the Creed by heart.

As regards profound reflection upon divine things, the opinion of the Order was that general in the early Middle Ages: "Alas for thee, poor doubter, thou art indeed forlorn, and sooth to say 'twere better if thou hadst ne'er been born." After a secret trial, a count of Nassau was sentenced to imprisonment for life "because he was a doubter." Being fully aware of the dangers of thought, the Order frankly disapproved of learned monasticism. It would not tolerate the Benedictines, the cultural aristocracy among the religious brotherhoods, putting up only with the Cistercian monasteries at Oliva and Pelplin because they had been founded by the princes of Pomerania; but no objections were lodged against the mendicant friars, who were ignoramuses. In this essentially political world, only one science was diligently fostered, that of historiography. The chroniclers of the Ordensland can worthily take their places among the best of medieval times: to mention only Peter von Dusberg who, at the beginning of the fourteenth century, described with the enthusiasm of a crusader the Order's campaigns in Old Prussia; and Johann von Pusilge who, a hundred years later, wrote his *Annals* with the liberal outlook of a citizen of the world, and his gaze fixed upon remote political vistas. Such accounts of the great deeds of the Teutonic Knights were sometimes read aloud in the refectories. No doubt amid the storms of frontier-life regular annalism was impossible. Poesy, like science, was little cultivated in the Ordensland. Rarely, too, in this arid atmosphere, was there any blossoming of the plastic arts, though these, perhaps, are somewhat less contributory to spiritual ennoblement. The period when they flourished most in Old Prussia was coincident with the political glories of the days of Winrich von Kniprode. The most impressive among the secular buildings of the German Middle Ages was finished under that exceptionally able Grand Master. I speak of Marienburg Castle, whose roots, whose vast cellarages, according to popular belief, were thrust as far below the surface of the earth as its pinnacles scaled the heavens. After dark, the light from its refectory windows shone wide over the country, being visible far up the Vistula, whose lower reaches, thanks to the cultural work of the Order, have been decorated with a more splendid setting than those of any other German river. For a long time before this, on the right bank of the Nogat, behind the stables, workshops, and other outbuildings of the Vorburg, protected by a chain of bastions and trenches, had stood the Grand Master's castle, with its chapter-house and the palace-church. The colossal mosaic statue of the Blessed Virgin, holding a lily by the stem, betokened that here was the acropolis of the religious State; and the deceased members of the knighthood had been laid to their last rest beneath the walls. Beside this sedate and solemn building was erected during Winrich's Grand Mastership the splendid Mittelschloss, the prince's cheerful secular residence, with the graceful windows of the Master's summer hall facing the dawn, and the marvellously bold vaulting carried on a single mighty pillar, like a palm-tree sustaining its fronds. But this lively architectural structure was nowise discordant with the severe spirit of the militarist State. Not only did wisely planned subterranean passages and the covered way which ran round the roof show that all was designed for defensive purposes. The chastity of the brickwork (a chastity elsewhere forgotten till recent times) indicated a seriousness unusual in the Gothic style. The sides of the windows were perfectly straight, for there was no recourse to decorative ornamentation; the surface of the walls was unadorned, save for a variegated colouring of the bricks to mitigate uniformity. The same restrained purity was characteristic of the accessory structures, down to the heavy towers rising out of the depths that housed the unmentionable privy. We must not attribute this extreme sobriety to the intrinsic poverty of a brick building. Another edifice built by the Teutonic Knights, ashlar this time, St. Elizabeth's Church at Marburg, shows the same modest reserve in the use of decoration. On the other hand arabesque inscriptions and many other peculiarities of the Order's architectural style betray the influence of Sicily and the East. Just as the Grand Master's castle became the model for all the strongholds of the Teutonic Knights; and just as many of them display with military precision the same sort of brickwork, so likewise is the severe character of the architecture repeated in the town houses. Who is not familiar with the aspiring boldness, the dignified seriousness, of the gabled residences with their prominent annexes that abound in the Langgasse of Danzig? The cathedral at Marienwerder rises like a fortress above the flats of the Vistula, and was repeatedly used as such by the dauntless burghers.

Though we cannot but be dazzled by the unparalleled and bold rise of the Order's power to giddy heights, still we feel that so premature a success must have lacked the requisites of stability. In accordance with one of the formidable laws which control the history of our race, it has rarely happened that at the core of human greatness the germs of decay have been more abundantly present than they were in the case of this State so full of contradictions. The Teutonic Knights were only able to command an abundance of talent because they were continually recruiting their ranks from the German nobility. Masterless blades were eager to join the Brotherhood because as the royal families and the towns elsewhere in Germany grew stronger there was little hope for such men as these to rise. Those who were stirred by profound religious instincts, and those bold spirits that were attracted by the lure of ambition, naturally turned towards the sole place where one born among the minor nobles might have hope of rising to a princely throne. But for that very reason the Order's future depended upon what happened to be the position of the aristocracy at any moment in the Empire it could not expect to control. Nothing but the sanctity of ecclesiastical discipline endowed the Teutonic Knights with the energy that enabled them in stateless days to preserve the majesty of the State. But the more fully the consolidating State became aware of its secular aims, the more oppressive seemed the ecclesiastical forms that were an essential part of its nature. Superficially regarded, the rule of this league of knights had nothing anomalous about it in times when it was usual to achieve important political aims by the united energies of corporations. But though we must praise the Order posthumously for having left nothing to occur by the simple power of organic growth, being determined to arrange everything in accordance with its own inviolable will, we must remember that it was rigid and inalterable, so that at a time when all was changing among its subjects, it met attempts at internal reform by a theocratic "non possumus." Thus was a great gulf fixed between rulers and people when among the grandchildren of the first settlers a sentiment of Prussian patriotism began to develop, and the disgruntled aboriginal Prussians realized that their destinies were being decided by a circumscribed caste of homeless aliens. The immigrants and the offspring of permanent settlers were soon as mutually antagonistic as in Spanish America at a later date were the European-born and the Creoles. Indeed matters were even worse in Old Prussia, where the celibate German seignior was bound by no domestic tie to the subjugated country. It is true that the Order offered free scope to every man of exceptional energy, but only if he would take the vows that entitled him to the privileges of the organization. The independents among the gentry, unless sworn to chastity, were excluded from independent political activity. The very Order which regarded the burghers of Lübeck and Bremen as brothers, showed theocratic mistrust by debarring the nobles of the country from entry. With frigid rationalism it might adopt every new political notion to which the times gave birth, but the basis of its constitution remained immutable. The monarchical idea, the only one that could lead the peoples of the Middle Ages on to enduring civilization, the idea whose redemptive qualities were being tried in France as early as the opening of the fifteenth century, could find no place in the Ordensland so long as the religious faith of the people made them regard as criminal the secularization of religious States.

That faith had indeed been long since undermined. At no time had the inhuman doctrine of the mortification of the flesh secured universal assent among the Germans, in whom the joy of life was strong. It was not merely a gross sensuality that revived in the early Middle Ages, but also a less questionable and more unprejudiced view of the sexual life. "Woman's beauty holds man's eyes, and sinful though it be, this need cause no surprise," says a cheerful German lilt. The Teuton who had once been forbidden to kiss even his mother, had been "corrupted" by association with crusaders who had learned from the heathen. The old prohibitions were being disregarded. Many a whisper from the retired cells of the fortresses had come to the ears of the common people. The white cloak of a knight vowed to chastity might often be seen in the forbidden quarters of the pleasure-loving cities; and a proverb was current warning the careful husband to keep his back door locked lest a brother wearing the black cross should steal in by night. The mocking disrespect of the folk for rulers who had lost the odour of sanctity, showed that the force of theocracy was in the long run tolerable only to those whose minds had been lulled into day-dreams by an unspiritual creed. When in the Empire the power and the moral stamina of the princes and the burghers were beginning greatly to surpass those of the nobles, the decay of the latter estate could not but affect the far-away settlement in the Ordensland. The more the prestige of the aristocracy declined, the more authoritative became the white-cloaked brethren towards all those who wore grey mantles. A draught, shameless and cheerless, was blowing athwart the hallowed refectories. The knights, who had had no experience of serious warfare since the days of the Battle of Rudau, filled in their time with idle boasting about the invincible strength of the weapons of the Order. The junkers, in their arrogance, spoke disdain-fully of the thoughtful Grand Masters who, having a keen grasp of the dangers of the period, were tempering the old policy of conquest. When at length, by a tragical fate which no foresight could have averted, this policy of conquest (essential to the Ordensland) had to be resumed, the German nobles experienced a pitiable disaster upon the very soil where they had once achieved their most signal triumphs.

Meanwhile the hothouse atmosphere of the colony was intensifying the hatred which the recently subjugated people, unused to piety, felt for its foreign masters. The German overlords necessarily seemed alien to the Old Prussians in days when the aversion of the indigenes was undergoing a regrettable development. Two new aristocracies had come into being beneath the dominant caste, and they were more closely connected with the country than were the Teutonic Knights. The leading urban families, notably the Fervers, the Letzkaus, and the Hechts, who were all influential in Danzig, had long been discontented with the harshness of the government. Here we again encounter one of the disastrous contradictions in the make-up of the Order. Only because it was a great purchaser could it entertain the scheme of undertaking a commercial policy upon the grand scale; but the fact that it pursued trade on its own account could not but alienate the burghers. Among the landed gentry, especially the well-to-do Renys' and Kynthenaus of Kulmerland, there now originated the

Lizard League. The members of the League were vowed to devote bodies and wealth to attacking all adversaries on behalf of any honourable purpose—all adversaries "except our sovereign lords." But who could tell what plans were discussed behind this mask, at secret meetings? Nor could the Order rely upon the safeguard of monarchical authority, or upon the loyalty of the lower classes—least of all at this turn from the fourteenth century to the fifteenth, when storm was in the night air, heralding the dawn of modern civilization. In this unhappy generation everything holy was being desecrated. Dante's prophecy of a hundred years earlier, "the Roman See, because it combines within itself two authorities, will fall into the mire," was being horribly fulfilled. Two Popes were quarrelling for the triple crown, two Emperors for the sceptre of the world, with the result that the heathen said mockingly: "Now the Christians have two Gods, and if one will not forgive them their sins, they can apply to the other." Christ's vicegerent was chased along the highway, and the mercenary general from Naples hitched his charger to the altar at St. Peter's. Not long before this the Black Death had been raging, and in many of the cities the Jews were burned, on the ground that they had caused the pestilence, while the "Lord have mercy" of the flagellants, the penitential song of guilt-burdened mortals, rang through the streets.

With ferocious scorn the poor began railing against the sinful lives of the rich. "Strumpets," screamed the crowd, "come to the town-council out of the forbidden streets, to complain of the councilmen's daughters; saying that these girls are spoiling their trade." While the chiefs of Christendom were making ready to restore peace of mind to their flocks by reforming the Church root and branch, the political structure of the old world was getting out of gear.

Vanished was the reverence of the impoverished for the old order. In France, the Netherlands, and High Germany the peasants were rising in revolt, while from England there now sounded for the first time the fierce question of Wat Tyler and his followers—the cry which will ever be repeated so long as the untutored natural energy of the ill-treated masses makes them rebel against the artificiality of an outworn civilization: "When Adam dalf and Eve span, who was then the gentleman?" In Prussia, likewise, an unruly spirit stirred, so that the Teutonic Knights thought it expedient to forbid public meetings and armed gatherings. A good while earlier the new forces of the people had made effective use of their weapons. It was a century since 8,000 pairs of golden spurs had been stored in Courtrai church, but in 1302 a Flemish weaver, nicknamed "Peter the King" and John Breydell, butcher of Bruges, raised a citizen army which defeated the French chivalry and carried off these boastful trophies. With spiked maces the Switzers, and with long pikes the Ditmarsh peasants, were able to defy the knightly art of war; while the Bernese sang triumphantly of their victory at Laupen, "'twas there we made Count Rudolf scream." It was at the opening of the fifteenth century that Emperor Ruprecht's army of knights had to retreat, "despoiled, shamed, and scorned," after a crushing defeat at Brescia by the Roman mercenaries. Long since, in fact, had the Order become painfully aware that a new estate of warriors had begun to exist. The urban civilization of the time was becoming more and more estranged from the knights-errant that wore the cross; and the songs of such innovators as Heinrich von Teichner now made mock of the "Prussian crusaders," who gained by their long journeys nothing more than the untutored admiration of the crowd, which cried: "Look what a distance he has ridden." Only the exceptionally pious in the Empire continued, for the good of their souls, to send mercenaries to Prussia. Soon even this source of reinforcements dried up, and, like other States, the Order was compelled, at vast expense, to recruit as nuclei of its armies the drilled infantry and the lavishly paid archers of Genoa. This change in the methods of warfare proved in the long run more suitable to a national economy than had been the costly war-making of earlier days. For the nonce, however, even the Teutonic Knights' well-filled treasury was almost emptied by the unanticipated expenditure. Many less prosperous States were eliminated from the number of the great powers, and the sovereignties of Europe became a more select circle. But, above all, it was an absurd, and soon an intolerable circumstance that a league of knights should have to conduct its campaigns with the aid of mercenaries.

At a time when from the Holy Empire there once more sounded Walther von der Vogelweide's refrain, "leaky is my roof, crumbling are my walls," the scattered forces of the Slavs were being ominously reconcentrated, and were marshalling themselves with deadly menace against the Germans. The Hussite movement was already beginning in the bosom of the most talented of the Slav peoples. Chased away by the national fanaticism of the Czechs, the German students fled from Prague to Leipzig, and for a long period the capital of Bohemia remained the chief educational centre for all the Western Slavs. At about the same time, Grand Duke Jagiello of Lithuania, an ambitious and exceptionally able prince, had ascended the Polish throne. Within four days he inflicted two terrific blows on the Order by undergoing baptism on February 15, 1386, and marrying the heiress to Poland on February 18, 1386. When the Grand Duke had the

sacred fire of the heathen gods extinguished in the
Castle of Wilna, and decided that the consecrated
serpents were to be put to death, it followed as a matter
of course that all those in his realm who had hitherto
been enemies to Christ must, like himself, accept the
new religion. If the persuasion of the recently ordained
priests, who offered woollen mantles, proved in-
efficacious, the peasants were driven into the rivers for
baptism by thousands at a time! Thus was undermined
the Teutonic Knights' shrewd policy of conquest.
How could the Order count any longer upon the access
of foreign knights as war-guests, now that its neighbours had all become Christians, and what had
previously been crusades were ordinary secular
campaigns? Having been elected king of Poland under
the name of Wladislaus II, the new monarch enhanced
the privileges of the nobles by conferring extensive
rights on them, and tried to mitigate the Germano-
phobia of the implacable junkers by promising to bring
back under Polish rule the provinces that had been
detached, especially Pomerellen.   The unhappy
disputes in the Lithuanian ruling house were appeased
when Wladislaus, in 1392, appointed his cousin
Witowt (or Witold) Grand Duke of Lithuania. Thus
was effected what had long been aimed at, a close
alliance between Lithuania and Poland, with the
result that the Order, whose primary object was the

conversion of the heathen, was now confronted by a foe no less rigidly Catholic than itself, and this double realm speedily advanced its frontiers far into Podolia, until it nearly reached the Black Sea. At this time the Hanse towns were engaged in a quarrel about the privileges of Lübeck. As regards their internal condition they were weakened by the enmity between the junkers and the guildsmen, and they looked on inertly while at Kalmar, in 1397, under the strong hand of Margaret, queen of Denmark, the three northern crowns were united. The Teutonic Knights were speedily to be made aware of the intensified self-confidence of its neighbours. The Samaites, who had so recently been detached from Lithuania, rose in rebellion, behaving "like young wolves which, when well fed, are all the readier to attack those who tend them." Memel was stormed by the barbarians, and not till 1406, when nearly ten years had elapsed, was the Order able to re-establish its rule over the town. In this perilous situation, the Knights thought it expedient to protect their rear, so in 1408 they ceded Gottland to the queen of the North. It was plain enough that the idea of an independent naval policy, however splendid, remained impracticable so long as nothing could be achieved in the way of remoulding the constitution of the league of heavily armed riders by the extensive inclusion of mobile democratic elements. Anyhow the sop thrown to Scandinavia could do little good while the power of King Wladislaus was growing so formidable. Profiting by his study of the policy of "divide and rule" which the Knights had hitherto applied against Poland and Lithuania, the king took a leaf out of their book and adopted the same method against them. The clergy of Livonia, perpetually discontented, openly asked for the support of the Poles against their Teutonic overlords; and in Prussia it was currently reported that secret messengers often came from Cracow to collogue with the Lizard Knights of Kulmerland. The minor Wendish princes of Pomerania were ready to acclaim the new greatness of the Slav king. Wladislaus' ambitions were not confined within the frontiers of Christendom, for he entered into an alliance with the heathen Tartars and Wallachians. The German seigniors could not but regard this as recklessly criminal, but the policy commended itself easily enough to a king of Poland, for a motley mixture of Ruthenians and Saracens, of Armenians and Tartars, dwelt in the south-eastern corner of this quasi-Christian borderland—a mish-mash of peoples that betokened the proximity of the Orient. Thither, too, since the days of Casimir the Great, masses of the Jews driven out from Germany had migrated, and among this medley of Christians and Pagans, of Jews and schismatics, even Wladislaus, though a good Catholic, could not afford to despise the aid of the heathen.

Thus in the very period when the Ordensland was acquiring its greatest dimensions, the moral foundations of its dominion were being undermined, the power of its irreconcilable enemies was growing, and the menaced State could expect no help from the tottering Empire. Almost inevitable seems a comparison with the situation of the new Prussian militarist kingdom during the two decades that followed the death of Frederick the Great. War had for some time been imminent. The princes of Pomerania, incited by the Poles, were blocking the roads along which warriors might have moved to the help of Prussia; and King Wladislaus forbade his merchants to carry on trade by way of the Ordensland. It came to blows, at last, when the Knights acquired the important waterway of the Netze at Driesen to improve their communication with Neumark. In 1410, Grand Master Ulrich von Jungingen, a belated representative of the old knighthood, moved southward at the head of the mightiest army the Order had ever called to the colours. With the foolhardiness of a knight errant, he staked all upon a single throw of the dice. Under sixty-five banners, fifty thousand men advanced, a full third of them mounted, and the heavy guns of Marienburg were actually taken along into the field. On July 15th (the anniversary of the day on which the apostles separated for their mission journey into the world), at Tannenberg Heath the Knights joined battle with a force twice as large as their own, the united strength of the two eastern powers. With chivalric arrogance they refrained from a surprise attack on the Poles, and challenged them to open combat. The Lithuanians had already been defeated, and the men of the black cross had begun triumphantly to sing "Christ is risen!" But Wladislaus' commander-in-chief, little Zyndram, seized his opportunity when the Knights' left wing in reckless disorder was pushing its attack. He flung his forces against the main body of the German army, being boldly supported by Johann Ziska, leader of the Bohemian mercenaries, this being the first occasion on which Ziska made his name a terror to his deadly enemies, the Teutons. When, now, the Lizard Knights of Kulmerland treacherously lowered their flag, the result was the first signal victory gained by the Slavs over our nation. The slaughter was unexampled in the history of the north. Innumerable corpses—tradition says a hundred thousand—were strewn upon the field; the flower of the German nobility perished; of the great chiefs of the Order only one escaped death; while the Tartars and the Cossacks practised their hideous tricks of mutilation upon the Grand Master's body.

After his victory, King Wladislaus had twenty-one German banners to hang up in Cracow Cathedral. Jan Dlugosz (better known in the west under his Latinized name Johannes Longinus), the famous Polish historian who was born five years after the Battle of Tannenberg, described the trophies in his great work, and even now, centuries later, Slav folk-songs are to be heard that recount the most glorious day in the annals of Polish arms.

But while the cautious elderly king remained with his weakened army for days on the battlefield, while the heads of the captured grandees were being struck off by the axes of his executioners, and while the wine seized in the Knights' camp was being abundantly consumed by the victorious Poles, there arose from among the ruins of the Order the second of its great men, Heinrich von Plauen. They all resembled one another, just as they all sported rampant lions in their coats of arms, these Heinrich Plauens, members of that House of imperial bailiffs which has now become that of the princes of Reuss—a race of tough masterful men, animated by royal ambition, but harsh and unamiable, with a cold insight into essentials. Long ere this they had made it a practice to send their bravest sons into the Order, and once before, at the Battle of Plowce, a Plauen among the Teutonic Knights had stabilized the fortunes of war. Hardly had the news of the disaster at Tannenberg reached the young Commander of Schwetz, who was at the western frontier keeping watch on the princes of Pomerania, than he realized how the fate of the centralized States would be determined by the fate of Marienburg. So he garrisoned the fortress with 3,000 men, saw to the condition of its walls, and set fire to the sumptuous town of which it formed the core—lest the Poles should find easy shelter there. But within a month the whole country had dishonourably and law-lessly surrendered to King Wladislaus, who at length retired to the north—for all were allured by the promise of Polish freedom (read, anarchy), saying: "Just this would Antichrist do, in such wise make subject unto himself those whom he cannot otherwise compel." The bishops, glad to be freed from the strict supervision of the Order, set a pernicious example; and the indiscriminate cowardice of those who remained in charge of the strongholds drove into the Polish camp many a man who would, but for that, have remained staunch. It seemed as if all was up with the Order; its army had been hopelessly beaten, and the treason of the refugees carried off its treasures into the Empire. The Danzig town council formally welcomed the Polish captain, who entered the city to the accompaniment of trumpets and kettledrums, while the Knights of Kulmerland sent threatening dispatches to the defender of Marienburg. "May God never forgive them," writes the chronicler; for this was an act of treason of the most wicked kind, unparalleled even in days when turncoats were common. Well might the people whisperingly declare that the Blessed Virgin herself had appeared in the ranks of the Teutonic overlords, dazzling the Poles; and that this was why, amid so much baseness, Marienburg had been able to hold out, against superior forces, and even against its own artillery which the enemy had captured at Tannenberg and now used against it. Dysentery was raging in the king's camp; and "the longer he stayed to besiege, the less could he effect." After his repeated futile attempts to take the place by storm, the insubordinate Sarmatian spirit came to the front once more, and the monarchy had not sufficient authority to keep the Polish nobles under the colours. The Lithuanians refused to go on fighting—at least, such is the version of the Poles, who wished to escape blame for their failure. Anyhow, after two months Wladislaus raised the siege. This unexpected success inspired the loyal in the country with fresh hope, and one fortress after another pledged its faith to the new Grand Master. When towards the close of the year King Sigismund of Hungary threatened to invade Poland, Wladislaus hastened, at the beginning of 1411, to sign the peace of Thorn, as the result of which everything reverted to the condition that had prevailed before the war, except that the territory of the Samaites went back to Lithuania for the Grand Duke's lifetime.

A few months earlier, Plauen had made obeisance in King Wladislaus' tent, having gone thither to beg peace from the arrogant conqueror. But now he was once more ruling a larger domain than that over which Grand Master Winrich had formerly held sway. Yet how different was his lot from his predecessor's. Winrich had been easily and happily sustained by waves of happiness, whereas the ill-fated Plauen was unceasingly and ineffectively struggling against a terrible doom. Being clear-sighted, he could not fail to be aware that the boon of peace had come to him by chance alone. The chapel he built at Tannenberg was to keep the Order in mind of the day of defeat, and of the need for further struggles. An exorbitant debt, the cost of ransoming the prisoners, lay upon the land which had been devastated by the Hunnish wrath of the foe. A tenacious will that was to know nothing of forgiveness must prevail in a country which twice within a few weeks had been forsworn. Wrathfully did the Grand Master himself break the oath taken on signing peace, to the effect that the past would be forgotten and forgiven—for the Brethren who had taken refuge in the Empire were brought back in chains. When he mustered the unfortunates who were left in what had once been a great Order—undisciplined and disobedient youths who had not known its flourishing days, and a handful of outworn elders whose daily prayer was for release from the burden of office—in the mind of him who became friend to Frederick, sixth burgrave of Nuremberg and first Hohenzollern elector of Brandenburg, in the mind of the proud man who had witnessed the revelation of the Blessed Virgin to the German ranks at Marienburg, there now ripened the bold idea that the Order's original statutes had been invalidated by its heinous crimes, and that henceforward the Redeemer's will must alone prevail among the disloyal.

Though he thus disregarded the ancient laws of the decaying Order, as a sagacious statesman he recognized that the time had come for granting to the comparatively fresh energies of the nobility and the towns a right to participate in political affairs. That was why in 1412 he summoned an assembly of delegates from the cities and the aristocracy which was to vote supply and give approval to or withhold approval from any important legislative proposals. This was a most arbitrary step, inasmuch as the regulations of the Order expressly forbade any such intervention on the part of laymen; but it had become necessary because unexampled demands had now to be made. Fortune had frowned on the gloomy ruler, pestilence and failure of the crops were destroying whatever the Cossacks had spared, and twice a levy was needed upon everyone down to the maids and the monks. The people could not but regard their harsh ruler as a foolhardy innovator, this being witnessed by the traditional description of Plauen as a favourer of Hussite heretics. Several risings had to be savagely repressed. Lizard Knights and German seigniors had vowed to take the Grand Master's life, and the conspirators were ruthlessly punished. Wealthy Danzig, which of late had become aware of its own power, refused to pay the new tax, walled up the entrance from the town into the keep, and built a strong tower, the "Kitchen Squint," from which the burghers could see what food was being prepared for the Brethren. At length the dictatorial Commander (Heinrich von Plauen's brother) had some notables of the council put to death without trial—a crime which the embittered burghers could not easily forget. But the Grand Master did not punish the Commander. Instead he nominated a new town council composed of supporters of the Order. Meanwhile, as a side issue, were going on acrimonious disputes with the expelled bishops who had headed the great treason, but demanded reinstatement now that peace had been secured. Plauen bluntly refused "to foster vipers in his bosom or to kindle a fire in the bows of his own ship."

Thus did the Grand Master pass two anxious years. The pitiable confusion of the Ordensland convinced King Wladislaus that to make peace with it had been foolishly premature. In fact (no matter what sapient scholars may say to the contrary), there is truth in the old tradition that the decay of the Order dates from the Battle of Tannenberg. Thenceforward the Germans were no longer supreme over the western Slavs, for the Teutonic Knights had forfeited the prestige of invincibility which is half the power of a militarist State. The Ordensland, being surrounded by Catholic countries, was in no better position than other German territories. Such foreign visitors as continued to make their way into Prussia could only dilate upon what they regarded as the impregnability of its fortresses; and towards the end this defensive power of a land that had been sucked dry could only be maintained by funds derived from landed property within the Empire. Feeling sure of victory, therefore, Wladislaus began a policy of impudent violence. His captains undertook plundering raids across the Prussian frontier; Prussian merchants were taken prisoner upon the Polish highways; while the Grand Duke of Lithuania actually built the fortress of Welun upon the Ordensland's territory, and when a complaint was lodged he replied that the whole of Prussia had formerly been part of Lithuania. Plauen, however, still clung to peaceful

methods, and begged King Sigismund of Hungary to
mediate. But Sigismund forgot his duty to the Empire.
Just as later, to please the Danes, he repudiated
the German Schauenburgers' hereditary claim to
Schleswig, so now did he regard the quarrel between
the Germans and the Poles as a valuable opportunity
for enriching himself, and for this reason his mediation
came to naught.

Only then did the Grand Master, on his own
responsibility and without consulting his subordinate
officers or the country he ruled, decide in the autumn
of 1413 to break the peace that was no peace.   But
when he proposed this bold venture, there was one of
his principal subordinates, Chief Marshal Küchmeister
von Sternberg, who was confident that this generation
would not endure anything so outrageous.   A vigorous
and corpulent fellow, and one whose diplomatic
abilities were mediocre, Sternberg counted upon the
baser passions of men of his own type.   Nor was he
mistaken in his reckoning.   The Poles had already
invaded the Ordensland to attack the strongholds
which Plauen had taken care to have adequately
equipped, when the Chief Marshal forbade the Grand
Master's brother to advance.   The troops were ready
to obey the rebel, and the campaign was frustrated.
Thereupon Plauen, on St. Burkhard's day (October 14,
1413), summoned the Chapter to punish the mutinous

Chief Marshal. At this Chapter were present all those
who envied young Plauen for having risen over their
heads to the position of Grand Master, together with
the timid peace-at-any-price men, and those who had
been alarmed by Heinrich's readiness to use the mailed
fist. Sternberg had sufficient skill to guide these dis-
harmonious elements, and to induce them with unclean
hands to insist upon the strict letter of the law. The
result was that Plauen was deposed for having done his
utmost to save the Order—on the ground that his
action involved a violation of the statutes. Nevertheless in this lamentable Chapter so feeble and irresolute
were the younger men despite their hatred, and so
short-sighted were the elders in their compassion, that
to the scandalously maltreated and dangerous Plauen
was assigned the modest commandery of Engelsburg.
Thither went the discrowned Grand Master, still short
of middle age, to the tedious montony of a subaltern
post. Sternberg succeeded him as Grand Master; the
miscreants who had plotted Plauen's assassination were
pardoned; and the Ordensland, ruled by dullards and
poltroons, moved on inevitably towards destruction.
From the Empire came the denunciations his friends
uttered against the "perjured traitors" and what not—
but strong words were all that the Empire could offer.
At length, it would seem, the embittered mind of the
ill-used man became reconciled to the idea of doing

obeisance to King Wladislaus as he had done once before at Marienburg, in the hope of making his way back into the Grand Mastership under the protection of Polish arms. But a tragical destiny rendered it impossible for him to put this plan to the test, and thus show whether it was grandly or basely conceived. His brother's negotiations with the Poles were discovered, Heinrich von Plauen was charged with being a party to them, and in 1414 was put under strict confinement. A life that had appeared to be on the way to splendid heroism ended in detestable prose. For another nine years he had to endure a living death, and the letters are extant in which the "ex-Master" complained to the new authorities that his gaolers were intolerably sparing in their allowance of provender. Only in the evening of his days was he given a minor post, the office of warden at Lochstädt. But from that time the Order was dominated by so fierce a spirit of partisanship that the subsequent chroniclers of the Teutonic Knights had never a word to say about this great man's imperishable services, and spoke only of his harshness and his treason. The circumstances attending his ultimate fate are still wrapped in mystery. This much, at least, is clear, that his brother fled to Poland as a traitor, but the only evidence that Heinrich von Plauen, sometime Grand Master, had anything to do with the affair is that furnished by the accusations against him lodged

by some of Küchmeister's supporters. Little credence
need be placed upon the utterances of men as fanatical
and unconscientious as these were; and yet we are not
entitled to disbelieve them on the ground of the mere
supposition that such a hero can never have been a
traitor. Just as light-minded theologians are prepared
to base the idea of God upon mere negations, so in
history do we encounter the moral jejuneness of those
who conceive human greatness to be nothing more
than the antithesis to crime. Such question-begging
ignores the profound truth that every great man is no
less richly endowed for evil than for good.

After St. Burkhard's day, 1413, the last traces of
greatness vanished from the degenerate State. Only
now and again did a brave warrior emerge from the
ruck of the despised Order, which could no longer rely
upon the fresh energies of the Empire, but had in truth
become "the hospital refuge, and receptacle for
German progeny." In these same October days of
1413 the diet of Horodlo cemented the alliance
between Poland and Lithuania, accepted the
Lithuanian boyars into the kinship of the Polish nobles,
and reaffirmed the Catholic character of the duplex
realm. By repeated invasions of the Ordensland this
union continued to emphasize its sense of superiority.
Samaiten, Sudauen, and Nessau were ceded by the
Teutonic Knights in a series of disgraceful peace

treaties. Reviled by the Deutschmeister (this had now become the title of the head of the German possessions of the Order) for " the weak and contemptible way in which the enemy had been resisted," the militarist State assured the Emperor, the Pope, and the imperial council of its devotion to peace. Who could doubt this, now that a foe of such long standing as the Grand Duke of Lithuania had been accepted as a half-brother? No one could mediate in this unequal struggle. On the contrary, it was openly declared at the courts that the Order no longer had a place in the monarchical world, and would be better advised to transfer once more its border defence against the heathen to Cyprus or the Turkish frontier. It was a war of principles and nationalities. The fanatical alliance of the Slav peoples became more stalwart than ever. On the ground that "blood is thicker than water," the kings of Poland entered into a league with the Hussites and the princes of Pomerania. Polish negotiators were already preaching among the Prussians the Slav doctrine that Prussia was really a Polish country, as was betokened by its place-names. In verity, when at Taus and Tachau the nobles of the Empire were being battered to death by the flails of Hussite peasants, and when far and wide in Low Germany the fanfare of Bohemian trumpets was heralding death to all of German blood and all that wore spurs—a number of heretics whose primitive camps were laagers like those still seen among the Boers of South Africa raided the Ordensland, pillaged the monastery of Oliva, greeted the sea with a wild Czech song about "God's warriors," and filled their water-bottles with brine in token that the Baltic once more obeyed the Slavs, as of old it had obeyed them in the days of Otakar, King of Bohemia.

Yet this disastrous growth of the power of their hereditary foe did not lead to a moral strengthening of the Teutonic Knights, any more than it had had that effect upon the nobles of the Empire. Internal dissensions broke out anew. With the secret support of the rural districts and the towns, three assemblies simultaneously refused to obey the commands of the Chief Marshal; the Grand Master and the Deutschmeister were at odds. At length the Order ceased to have a strictly German character. The Danzig chroniclers blame Heinrich von Plauen ("God forgive him") because he had allowed other than pure North Germans to appoint him Grand Master. Thereafter within the Brotherhood the Low Germans began to rail against the Bavarians, Swabians, and Franconians, until, after a long and detestable wrangle, the Grand Master had to promise that his council should be made up by the same number of persons from each territorial division of the Empire. Amid these disputes, the freedom of the country became consolidated. The towns were beginning to make certain demands before they would pay homage to the Grand Master, and the land took sides in the quarrels among its German overlords. So completely had the centre of gravity shifted that in its new form (1430) the territorial assembly founded by Plauen had among its twenty-four members only six German seigniors. The unceasing conflicts were gnawing the very marrow of the Ordens-land, while excessive taxation and the arbitrariness of the Knights filled the burghers with bitterness. A number of unlucky accidents made things worse: a succession of bad harvests; the enigmatic failure, after 1425, of the herrings to turn up at the usual Hanse fishing-grounds off the coast of Scania. Law and order were unknown to the Prussians now that the Knights' patrols were unable to check the depredations of the rabble rout that had infested the roads since the war. The Poles, of course, did their utmost to promote discontent among the squires in the highlands and Pomerellen, whose forefathers a century earlier had enjoyed the anarchical liberty of the Polish nobles.

Out of such embitterment originated the presumptuous idea of forming a Prussian League, which came into existence in Marienwerder on March 14, 1440, at the diet attended by representatives from part of the knighthood and from the towns. A State

within the State, it professed at the outset to be designed
only to support everyone who wanted to secure his
rights, but it soon appointed a permanent privy council
and levied taxes from the leaguers. Its leading spirits
were the patriciate of Danzig and a South German
knight, Hans von Baisen by name, a crafty and
ambitious fellow who in early youth, at the court of
the great Heinrich von Plauen, had perceived the
weakness of the Order, and had now returned from
distant campaigns to find that his energies were rusting
under the rule of the Teutonic Knights. "A poisoned
lame dragon, a basilisk," we read of him in the
chronicles of the Order, "is the worst of all traitors."
The perfidious statecraft of incapable Grand Masters,
which first encouraged the League and then denounced
it to the Emperor, brought new adherents, and
facilitated its downward career. Two strangely mixed
motives were active in causing this movement: the
colony, now growing old, demanded (naturally enough)
independence, and that it should be freed from the
control of a State authority which was outworn; while
the restless common people were eager to be subject
only to the anarchical rule of the Poles. When, now,
in answer to the complaints of the Order, Emperor
Frederick III declared the League null and void
"because of its weakness and lack of dignity," with the
result that the Teutonic Knights were grateful to an

Empire they had coldly ignored in brighter days, the advocates of liberty ventured a last defiant crime. On February 4, 1454, the countryside and the towns repudiated allegiance to the Order, and a bedell of the council of Thorn brought the document to the Grand Master. "You have treated us as your property," said the leaguers, "but nature herself teaches everyone to revolt against the improper use of force, and to punish malefactors ruthlessly." The castle of Thorn, the first fortress that had been built among the heathen by the German conquerors two centuries before, was stormed by the raging mob. When beacons were lighted on the turrets, the whole country rose, and within a few weeks fifty-six strongholds were in the hands of the League. Already Baisen was on the way to Cracow to offer King Casimir IV the rule over Prussia, "which used to belong to the crown of Poland."

The king came, and there ensued widespread desertions like those which had followed the defeat at Tannenberg a generation before, but this time on an even larger scale. Some of the German seigniors actually paid homage to Casimir, for Poland was lavish with its privileges, allowing freedom of trade and the right to participate in the election of the monarch, while Baisen was made viceroy of Prussia. But a fierce civil war followed, for the loyal German magnates were in a fury with the "leaguer-curs" who had been corrupted by the "Lizard poison," while the Poles and the leaguers took up arms against the "religious bigots" of the Order, and also against the "perjured knaves" of townsmen who, after considerable hesitation, had once more espoused the cause of the Teutonic Knights. It was a case of "all against all." The burghers of the three towns of Königsberg fought savagely on the quays of the Pregel and in the waterways and the neighbouring alleys. At Danzig the guilds rose again and again in support of the Order, until at length the junkers got the upper hand, and the guildsmen who were taken prisoner were chained to the benches of the galleys. As the first outcome of "Polish freedom" a despotic rule of the nobles became established, for the new town of Danzig, which had been one of the Teutonic Knights' most flourishing creations, was ruined by the unquenchable envy of the patriciate of the old town. To safeguard their scandalous profits the junkers, the patricians of the House of the Round Table, were firm in their support of the king's cause. The Poles were able to defray most of the expenses of the war with money from Danzig, obtained by the sale of the patrician ladies' jewels.

This war dragged on for thirteen years, poor in heroic deeds, though horrors were rife. The Grand Master, Ludwig von Erlichshausen, was a weakling, but Heinrich Reuss von Plauen, the Head Almoner,

cut a better figure, being a worthy descendant of the
Grand Master of that name, and one whose boldness
at the Battle of Konitz revived some of the ancient
glories of the Teutonic Knights. But the Order found
a new enemy in its own mercenaries. To defray their
enormous cost the Grand Master pledged to the
soldiers more than twenty of his towns and castles,
including Marienburg itself. When their pay was long
overdue, the mercenaries, most of whom were Bohemian
heretics, boldly occupied this most important of their
guarantees, and the tragedy was hideously relieved by
the shameful uproar of the satire that ensued. The
lashes of the whips carried by the Hussites were freely
used on the backs of the magnates of the Order, in the
very passage where some of the most distinguished
heroes of earlier days had been laid to rest. The rough
fellows broke into the cells, tied up the knights, and
proceeded to cut off their beards. Finally, at Pentecost,
1457, the Grand Master was driven out of his desecrated
stronghold. On a skiff he drifted down the Nogat to
the Frisches Haff and thence made his way to Königsberg, where the compassionate town council sent a
bedell to him with a barrel of beer. The castle of
Marienburg and the other fortresses were sold by the
mercenaries to the King of Poland. But amid all these
disgraces, a valiant man once more came to the front.
This was Burgomaster Bartholomäus Blome, who

opened the gates of the town of Marienburg to Reuss
von Plauen. For three years Blome and Plauen, the
last heroes of the Ordensland, held the city against the
Poles who occupied the castle and were encamped
without the walls. Then they had to yield to a force
by which they were greatly outnumbered, and the
burgomaster was decapitated by the victors.

"As far as the eye could see there was neither a tree
nor a bush to which a cow could have been hitched."
The Order and the king alone had squandered no less
than sixteen million Hungarian florins upon this
deplorable war. "Persons disloyal to Our dear wife"
had even begun complaining to the king, "how
disastrously we have been misled by You and Your
advisers." None but the captains of the mercenaries
had profited by the fight, and they became the ancestors of some of the latter-day Prussian nobles. The
scandalous, almost incredible finish of the war showed
how both parties had been bled white. I refer to the
conditions of the Perpetual Peace signed at Thorn on
October 19, 1466. All the land westward of the Vistula
and the Nogat was assigned to Poland; also Kulmerland, Marienburg, Elbing, and the bishopric of
Ermeland, which thrust like a wedge into the eastern
part of Prussia. The Vistula had again become a Slav
river. But the greater moiety of the Grand Master's
eastern dominions was returned to him as a Polish

fief. "The Master and the Order and all their possessions will henceforward be for ever more so closely associated with the realm of Poland that the whole will form one body, a race and people united in friendship, love, and harmony." In the Polish diet the Grand Master was to sit at the king's left hand as "prince and counsellor of the kingdom of Poland," and half of the knightly German seigniors were to be drawn from among Poles of every class! Weeping, and with torn raiment, the unhappy Grand Master swore fealty to the Poles in the Guildhall at Thorn. Never did a great power come to a more pitiable end. The affair was not only an inextinguishable shame, but was a pledge impossible to fulfil, for this vassal of Poland was still to govern through the instrumentality of two independent German princes, the Landmasters of Germany and Livonia.

The Emperor and the Empire looked on inert while the impotence of a theocracy that had been too rigid and the lawless arrogance of the mercantile patriciates and the squires were betraying "New Germany" to the Poles. "Contemplate the wrong that has been done to your German nation and to the land where your forefathers settled," wrote the Grand Master to the German nobles. But these nobles had just been wasting their energies in a ruthless war against the towns. Discipline and community of spirit were un-

known to this decayed generation, whose only effective
passion seemed to be class hatred—such hatred as is
disclosed by scornful songs which the princes launched
against the burghers. Everywhere selfishness was
rampant. Not for a moment did it occur to the Landmaster of Germany that he ought to offer up his
wealthy estates in order to save the nucleus of the
Order's power. The Livonian branch of the Teutonic
Knights, peeved by the excessive demands of their
Marienburg brethren, had long been following their
own bent. They appointed their Landmaster without
regard to the wishes of the rest of the Order, and had
been granted exclusive control of the whole of Estonia,
where, and along the Dvina, they were unceasingly at
odds with their insubordinate vassals. Shortly before,
the Transelbian nobles, seduced by Denmark's lucre
and Denmark's pledges of liberty, had sacrificed the
hereditary rights of their ruling house and elected the
king of Denmark Grand Duke of Schleswig-Holstein.
Soon after this, the Hanseatic League, whose fate had
so long been linked with those of the Teutonic Knights,
suffered a deadly blow. The Muscovites made a
victorious entry into Novgorod, but the German free
State did not sound the tocsin, and when in 1492
Ivan III built the fortress of Ivangorod close to the
Gulf of Finland, to challenge the German Narva, a
new power, the Russian, had entered Baltic politics.

There was only one man in Germany, Frederick II, Elector of Brandenburg, who had enough statesmanlike sagacity to understand all that was implied by this decline of Germanism in the north and the east. He held his grip on the Mark, and designed to establish his dynasty along the shore of the Baltic, hoping that it would be a rampart of the Empire. By marriages and by pacts with Lauenburg, Pomerania, and Mecklenburg, he laid the firm foundations of a great future. He offered to expel the Danes from German soil if the Emperor would grant him Holstein. But Vienna preferred to cede the outlying parts of the Empire to a foreigner rather than to a Hohenzollern; Prussia also awoke to the nature of Frederick's ambitions. The elector had realized the weakness of the Order, and hoped to save the Ordensland for Germany by becoming its hereditary sovereign. But so bold a scheme was beyond his grasp. He had to content himself, in 1454, with buying Neumark when the Teutonic Knights were in great financial straits, and was thus at least able to save this appanage of the Marks from the grip of the Slavs.

"You may break the old treasure-chest of iniquities," exclaimed Reuss von Plauen, when the leaguers destroyed one of the fortresses of the Teutonic Knights, "but you may rest assured that your children's children will bewail your deed." His prophecy was fulfilled, for

the mutilated State continued to limp miserably along.
The reconstruction of the Order had become impossible, for the Landmasters of Germany and Livonia
rightly refused to obey a Grand Master who had
become a vassal of Poland, and the Deutschmeister
was solemnly invested as a prince of the Empire.
Unsuitable candidates were allowed to don the white
mantle, now that no one recommended by the
Emperor or one of his princes could safely be refused.
The utmost wisdom the Knights could conceive was
pitiful enough. They hoped to frustrate the scheme for
copiously diluting them with Poles, and to evade the
need that the Grand Master should pay homage to a
Slav monarch by leaving his post vacant as long as
possible. Vain was the endeavour. The rulers in
Cracow knew well enough that the Order was power-
less, and they had gone so far as to hope that the Grand
Mastership would be permanently in the granting of
the crown of Poland. Besides, now that Panslavism
had become instinctive it was felt that the approval of
any demands made by Russia would be preferable to
the abandonment of Polish supremacy over Prussia.
Against this strong determination, all that the Order
could do was look to Rome (which vacillated shame-
lessly between the Teutonic Knights and their enemies),
and rely upon the "brave words" of the Emperor—
who was content to say vauntingly "the ancient and

honourable order must stick to the Holy Empire and the German nation."

At length the notion of monarchy prevailed. In 1498 the Teutonic Knights chose Duke Frederick of Saxony as Grand Master, hoping that the power of the House of Wettin would strengthen the Order. At least the outward aspect of a monarchy had been gained. A temporal court pranked at Königsberg; and the new Grand Master's talk was authoritative, was princely. Whole commanderies were summoned, to keep up appearances; and the State was run by sovereign councillors and chancellors who were not even members of the Order. Civil government was all that the Commanders troubled to carry on, their religious functions being completely ignored. In a word, the vestiges of the Ordensland were on the way to transform themselves into a comparatively insignificant monarchical territory, like many another in the Empire. But the royal will of a monarch was still lacking. As happened much later in the great questions of German statecraft, so here on a small scale the Hohenzollerns were to win the game which the Wettins weakly lost. After Frederick's death, with the same end in view in 1511 Margrave Albert of Brandenburg-Anspach—a man of no more than mediocre talent, but inspired by the covetous ambition of his line—was chosen Grand Master. He was determined to renounce allegiance to

Poland, and indeed Emperor Max adjured him to disregard the terms of the Perpetual Peace. But since neither the Empire, nor Saxony, nor Brandenburg, was prepared to venture war against Poland, the Emperor at length sacrificed the harassed German colony to the advantage of his house. At Vienna in 1515 he signed a treaty with the queens of Hungary and Poland, guaranteeing to the Habsburgs succession to the thrones of Bohemia and Hungary, but subjugating Prussia once more to Poland in accordance with the stipulations of the Perpetual Peace. Danzig and Thorn were exempted from the authority of the newly constituted Imperial Chamber and were subordinated to the Polish law courts. When, thereupon, envoys from the Poles and the Knights, respectively, came before the Emperor at Augsburg to present their sides of the dispute, the Emperor listened graciously to what the Poles had to say, and would not allow the Order's representative to speak. All the Emperor's "brave words," to the effect that in temporal matters the Teutonic Knights were only concerned with the imperial will, had been merely designed to browbeat the king of Poland into signing the treaty which bestowed the heritage of the Jagiellos upon the House of Habsburg.

Though thus abandoned by the Empire, in 1519 the Grand Master nevertheless ventured upon the unequal struggle, and for the last time there flickered among the German nobles the spirit of the old chivalry. But the forces of the new time were speedily to quench the flame. Franz von Sickingen, unquestionably the last of the German knights, raised an army and sent his son Hans to the help of the Order, backed up by many excellent birds (as the new field-guns, noisy rather than effective, were then named in military language), the "Nightingale" and what not. But the Grand Master was not much good as a commander, and could make little use of this reinforcement. Having been defeated, he signed an interim peace, and sought further help from the Empire, going thither in person.

By now, at length, minds were sufficiently ripe to understand another concept in virtue of which alone monarchy could be established in Prussia: the thought of secularization. Why was fate so unkind as to prevent the Ordensland entering the bright days of the Reformation as a mighty religious State, and then promptly transforming itself into a powerful secular realm? Certainly the political structures of the Old Church must have decayed and fallen into contempt before the audacious plan of secularizing the sacred could be vigorously entertained. The Prussians had long since become aware that the holy fraternity of

Teutonic Knights was, in truth, anything but holy, so they eagerly accepted the new faith. On Christmas Day, 1523, in the cathedral of Königsberg, Georg von Polenz, bishop of Samland, announced to his congregation the delight he felt "that Our Lord had for a second time been born upon earth." He was the first prince of the Catholic Church to accept Protestantism. A year later the first printing-press was set up in Prussia. The spiritual movement that was going on in the old homeland had powerful effects upon the distant colony. The German seigniors in Prussia were already beginning to obey the preachers of the reformed religion. Guttersnipes were prone to deride those who wore the white mantle of the Order. Many of the Knights voluntarily discarded the monkish habit. The Grand Master, even, when making his petitionary journey through the Empire, came in contact with the spirit of the new time. Nicholas Osiander appealed to his conscience. When he was in Wittenberg, Luther exhorted him to avoid spurious chastity, and to embrace the true chastity of marriage. The Reformer issued an admirable pamphlet addressed to the Teutonic Knights. Unsparingly he disclosed the falsehood that lay hid in the heart of the Ordensland: "A strange religious Order, this, formed to make war on the infidel. Why should it be secular, and wield a material sword? Nevertheless it claims to be a spiritual, a religious, body. How can these contradictions be reconciled? The Grand Master should set us a good example by establishing a straightforward dominion, one which, without cant or humbug, might be pleasing to God and the world."

The plain truth of such reasoning was conformable to the Grand Master's dynastic aims. He adopted his people's new faith, and by the treaty of Cracow, signed on April 8, 1525, was granted the land of Prussia as a temporal hereditary duchy in fee to his uncle King Sigismund. This was conceded on the ground that "all wars and disputes between the Poles and the Prussians have resulted from the fact that Prussia has not yet had a monarch ruling it properly by hereditary right." Most of the Teutonic Knights gladly accepted the new order of things; only a few clung firmly to Roman Catholicism, and above all (with the rigid conservatism of his House) a Heinrich Reuss von Plauen. The chief subordinate ruler of the Knights became the new duke's prime minister. The black cross vanished from Duke Albert's coat-of-arms, but the country's black eagle remained, adorned with an S (Stipendiarius) to indicate that Poland was its overlord. The Ordensland, as such, ceased to exist. All the same, this inglorious end was the modest beginning of a healthy development. Now that the State had frankly recognized its secular nature, it gained sufficient energy to progress, and to adapt

itself to changes in temporal affairs. A fresh stream of
German culture flowed through this border country as
soon as the new duke had founded Königsberg
University, the Albertina. Luther thankfully wrote:
"See the miracle that is being worked; with all sails
set, the word of God is speeding into Prussia." But the
religious vesture which Prussia had so boldly doffed
continued to exist in ghostly fashion. The duke
incurred the Pope's anathema and the Emperor's ban.
The Teutonic Knights in Germany repudiated the
action of the Grand Master, whom they regarded as a
traitor, and they issued revised statutes for the vestiges
of the Order. Thenceforward the new Grand Master
and the new Landmaster of Germany dwelt in the
south-west, the classical home of decayed spiritual
sovereignties. The German seigniors led the futile
existence of distinguished monks, and shut themselves
away from the healthy energies of the nation by insist-
ing upon proof of nobility, of which the Order had
known nothing in its palmy days. Irreconcilable and
unteachable, after the theocratic manner, they continued for centuries to demand the surrender of Prussia
by the wrongful, however illustrious, "dententores."
The court of Vienna often fostered a hope that the
glories of the Order would one day be revived in the
land where heresy had unfortunately come to prevail,
and the first king of Prussia could not but smile at the

noisy protests which the Order and the Pope uttered against him for having so presumptuously assumed royal dignity. The slothful court of Mergentheim was also unaffected by the storms of the revolution, for in the Promised Land of historical relics the caricature of ancient greatness was resurrected. There, at the very foot of the sunny vineyards, is a splendid castle of the Teutonic Knights, its gates adorned by the black cross in the Habsburg-Lorraine coat-of-arms.

Prussia had been subdued by the Poles. Now, far to the east, German territories were exposed to the onslaughts of the Muscovites. What a sinister development. Russia, the natural ally of the Prussians against the Poles, was irrevocably hostile to the Germans of Livonia, and co-operation of the Order with these brethren beside the Dvina had become impossible. Add the disharmony and weakness of the Holy Empire, the faulty policy of the Habsburgs, and the commercial rivalry of our Wendish towns (which refused to allow the Livonians free passage through the Sound, and applied to Riga and Reval the monopolist methods England was subsequently to employ with equal success against its North American colonies). For a time the towns in the Gulf of Riga flourished as the heirs of the commercial greatness of Novgorod. In its declining years the Livonian Order could still treasure the memory of its first hero, Walther von Plettenberg, who in 1502 beside Lake Pskow near the town of that name (still fighting on his knees when sorely wounded, as the legend runs) defeated the Muscovites, and thus secured half a century of peace for his country.

But the Master of the Livonian Order, not having wholly shaken off the influence of Roman Catholicism, was not sufficiently resolute promptly to follow the example of Albert of Brandenburg. Meanwhile Knöpken and Tegetmeier had brought to Livonia the Protestant faith and some knowledge of High German. But when the Master died, there ensued the devastating invasions of Ivan the Terrible, which resulted in a ferocious and sanguinary struggle with the Russians. Here, as in Prussia, the Germans weakened themselves by treachery and contentiousness, so that a Tartar chieftain could justly exclaim that they had made a halter with which to hang themselves. The Grand Master gained nothing by complaining to the Emperor that the terrible and mighty Muscovite was likely to establish himself on the Baltic. But Gotthard Ketteler, the Landmaster, was able to save Courland from destruction by taking it over as a secular duchy under the suzerainty of the Polish-Lithuanian crown (1561). This most charming of the Baltic territories now enjoyed a comparatively fortunate season, and even the non-Germans were benefited by Reymer's enthusiasm for the Letts, which induced him to translate the Psalms and the catechism, and thus make them acquainted with Lutheran doctrine. But for many generations Livonia and Estonia (where oppression of the peasantry was traditional) remained bones of contention among the northern powers. During these centuries of warfare the Baltic nobles became independent—a race which was tyrannical to its serfs, which was privileged by game-laws and in various other ways, and which clung tenaciously to its medieval hospitality towards guests and poor relations. They were Germans, doubtless, but the German they spoke was never vitalized by Luther, and became more and more impoverished; while their intellectual life was very inadequately nourished by the University of Dorpat, generously founded by Gustavus Adolphus.

At length it came to pass that a Livonian nobleman, Patkul by name, exasperated by the overbearing ways of the Swedes, once more invited the Russians into the country. Peter the Great and his wife (who succeeded him on the throne as Catherine I) subjected the Germans of Livonia to their rule. The new dominion brought the benefit of a long-desired peace; but this was the chief and perhaps the only advantage, for Russian propaganda undermined German civilization. The sins of the fathers were visited on the sons. Although more clement days had dawned, so that the nobles mitigated the burdens laid upon the serfs, the hatred they had aroused in their underlings was too deeply graven. The wiles of the popes [the parish priests of the Russian Orthodox Church] were successful in converting the Estonians and the Letts. As year followed year one who walked through the monotonous pine-forests came upon more and more Greek churches with their bulbous pinnacles. As before, in the whole countryside there were only three important towns. Almost the only remaining bulwark of Germanism was constituted by the right of the German barons to hold diets; and even though the fact that so many of the Baltic nobles had entered the service of the Russian State was, in some measure, a guarantee of the persistence of this aristocratic German institution, still the close association of the German nobles with the court of St. Petersburg tended to promote the Russianization of the province. The very name of the duchies was disused, and under Tsar Nicholas it seemed as if there must be truth in the servile complaint which at that time was sent from Dorpat to the Emperor: "For this is fate's undying will; where Russians are, lo all is still." In the reign of Nicholas' son and more gentle successor, Alexander II, German civilization thrived better in this region. The people began to drift back into the Lutheran Church it had so foolishly abandoned; German science flourished at Dorpat [Yuriev] University, which had been closed by Peter the Great in 1710, but was reopened by Alexander I in 1802 ; German education slowly advanced; and the relations between landowners and serfs improved. Since then, however, the evil days of oppression have returned, thanks to the excesses of a Panslavist Muscovite party, which expressly aimed at the destruction of the old-established Baltic territorial rights, and secured ample support from the fanatical equalitarianism of these democratic days and from the resurgent national sentiments of the Letts and the Estonians. In any case among all our German settlements those in the Baltic provinces of Russia are most imperilled. A small minority of Germans, no more than two hundred thousand among a total population of wellnigh two millions, must strive arduously, in very difficult circumstances, against powerful alien forces, and yet finds sufficient energy to send year by year men with a thorough German training into the interior of Russia. As far as royal Prussia was concerned, Danzig alone could rejoice in the new regime. The town junkers, the patriciate, favoured by the waywodes, could congratulate themselves on the wealth they derived from their monopoly of the Polish trade. The fame of the city became worldwide when Johann von Kolno, a Danziger, discovered [sic] Hudson's Strait and the coast of Labrador. At this period, during the Wars of the Roses, the German national pride of the Danzigers once more flamed high, when Paul Beneke, the Prussian Hanseatic hero, gained signal victories at sea over the English, and brought home valuable spoils—among them a precious picture of the Last Judgment (ascribed to Hans Memling), which is still held in high honour as the "Danzig Picture." The court of Cracow rewarded Danzig for its treason to Germany by special privileges, including the right of the city to add the Polish crown to its coat-of-arms. Once, however, it had to pay dearly for its misdeeds, for in 1526 the king of Poland instituted a bloody assize against the Lutheran faith. But ere long the Poles realized how earnestly the Germans had espoused the new doctrines, and were more tolerant lest they should lose their most important province. Danzig, therefore, was able to maintain itself as a wealthy free city even when the Hanseatic League had fallen a victim to Polish anarchy—much as Strasburg persisted independent under the Bourbons.

But the rest of the country suffered greatly from the Poles' shiftiness and from their deplorable incapacity as statesmen. The foundations of decent human behaviour were undermined, and German diligence vanished. Both in the upper and in the lower circles of Prussia, the conduct of the Polish diet was seduously imitated. The new rulers had but one aim—to uproot the German language, to get rid of German manners and customs. Marienburg was henceforward to be

known as Malborg; Kulm became Chelmo; while the
German noble families of Oppen, Hutten, Falken, and
Götzendorf, plumed themselves on being renamed
Bronikowski, Chapski, Plachecki, and Grabowiski.
The chartered territorial rights were swept away one
after another. Hans von Baisen, even, was so painfully
requited for the treason that had led him to seek
freedom from the enemy, that he died of a broken
heart. The office of royal gubernator was abolished;
Polish noblemen thrust themselves to the front as
waywodes, and succeeded one another as bishops of
Ermeland. A hundred years after the Peace of Thorn,
the diet of Lublin announced that the province had
been definitively incorporated into the realm of Poland;
the estates of Prussia were now to become part of the
diets of the nobles' republic. Two decades later Polish
was used as the official language even in the diets of
royal Prussia.

In very truth this unnatural state of affairs, that
Slavs should rule Germans, would have persisted, and
the work of Slavification would have been no less
successful in the towns of the Vistula valley than in the
open countryside, had not the Jesuits installed themselves in Poland and transformed it into a faithful
supporter of. Habsburg intrigue. Stanislaus Hosius,
active apostle of the Jesuits and leader of the Counter-
Reformation in Poland, got busily to work in Prussia

as well, and the theological academy at Braunsberg, known as the Hosianum, still keeps his memory green. But the towns of Prussia were supported in their resistance to priestly propaganda by some of the Polish nobles, who feared that the Society of Jesus might aim at getting possession of their landed property. After the Lublin diet, Achatius von Zehmen cried warningly to the Poles: "In days to come a potentate will deal with you no less violently than you are now dealing with the Prussians."

In the long run the conquest of royal Prussia was not advantageous to the Poles, for it introduced a new factor of resistance among the numerous discontented nationalities that were already smarting under the foreign tyranny of the Polish squirearchs. A Germano-Protestant community sense was still half-awake among the Prussian burghers, and throughout the dark days of Polish rule the German spirit would now and again manifest itself in some signal deed. At Frauenburg a German canon was thinking and investigating on every starry night throughout a generation, until at length there was revealed to him the convincing truth of what has become known as the Copernican system, and his name has been the pride of two hostile nations.

The essence of the desolating rule of the Poles is plainly disclosed by all that happened to Marienburg. Plundered and laid waste through occupation by the

Heyducks [Hungarian mercenaries], it passed finally into the hands of the Jesuits, and the civilized barbarism of the pious fathers completed what the rougher methods of the Heyducks had only begun. Jesuit architectural "improvements" were thrust in amid the sublime works of the Teutonic Knights, the fortress was surrounded by the dirty hovels of Scottish pedlars, and Jesuits were buried in the vaults of the Anna-Kapelle at the cost of violating the tombs of the Grand Masters. The Poles, distrusting the stability of the refectory pillars, filled in the spaces between them with thin walls, and the frankly simple brickwork was plastered over with lying stucco. Nor was the devastation rendered more pious when the magnificent Augustus the Strong came to visit a fortress whose greatness surpassed his understanding, and his inamorata Countess Cosel flaunted for a time her meretricious charms in the refectory which had once echoed to the clinking spurs of the Teutonic Knights.

In view of the oppressive and yet seductive neighbourhood of the great Slav realm, "where everything was noble," ducal Prussia—poor and depopulated, having only two seaports open to world commerce—could not possibly undertake the progressive statecraft that would have been appropriate to its heretical origin. Unruly, inspired by the old spirit of German insubordination and by fondness for aristocratic Polish anarchism, the Prussian nobles kicked against the control of feeble dukes and their favourites, held the rulers contentedly aloof from European trade, and only took up arms on the comparatively rare occasions when the serfs revolted against the exactions of the junkers, and had to be plunged into a blood-bath. The landed gentry and the proud patriciate of Königsberg held together like one man against the peasantry and the dependent towns. Protestantism had grown rigid, and assumed the lifeless form of Lutheran orthodoxy. The supporters of Melanchthon, who were favoured by the court, were threatened with the sword and with out-lawry. When the dukes forbade railing against Calvinism from the pulpits, the nobles induced their Polish overlord to cancel the prohibition, and to declare Calvin's doctrines devilish. All whose hearts were still animated by the contentious spirit of the Reformation sought refuge in foreign parts; the heroic family of the Dohnas quitted the inert and retired life of the province to take part in the religious wars of the Huguenots. It was the blossoming-time of Lutheran squirearchy; but here in Prussia, at one time the focus of the most intense German nationalism, things were now much more blatant than in the Marks, and the pride of the nobles produced no better results than crude turn-coatery. The provincial nobility "Polonized" again and again, holding truck with the Polish court, or at

Königsberg hospitably entertaining the Jesuits, whose help they wished as supporters against the princes. At their demand the crown of Poland willingly backed up their claims against their duke, and actually went so far as to summon Prussian diets in defiance of the latter's will.

More acrimonious, more unsparing, became the opposition of the nobility when the electoral house of Brandenburg, having first acquired the guardianship of the last duke of Ansbach, itself assumed the ducal dignity in 1618. It seemed to the Prussian aristocrats expedient, in the spirit of the most rigid particularism, to pursue the "policy of the fatherland" in opposition to the "despotism of the Mark of Brandenburg." Far too obtuse were these junkers to understand what a promising affair was the appearance of Gustavus Adolphus upon the scene. Vainly, in his most winning manner, did he point out that extreme measures had become necessary; and to those who defiantly spoke of Polish liberty he uttered the significant warning: "You may thank God that you are not direct subjects of Poland." It became known how the court of Vienna really hoped that ducal Prussia would become wholly subject to the crown of Poland; but the estates remained neutral in the world struggle. The country witnessed the utmost possible degradation of monarchy when George William of Brandenburg, running away from the German war, established his impoverished and undignified court in Königsberg.

But under his son there began at last to be fulfilled the foreboding of the Poles that if Prussia should pass into the hands of the House of Brandenburg this would mean the ruin of Poland. How much the Great Elector had to turn and twist to escape from his degrading position! Nothing but the grace of the king of Poland had made it possible for him to bury his father in accordance with Calvinist rites. His commissaries were refused audience of the estates of Prussia, being treated as the "envoys of a foreign potentate"; the towns closed their gates against his troops. But within a few years the despised vassal of the crown of Poland had become the pointer on the balance of the Polono-Swedish war. He had to avail himself of the most crafty diplomatic wiles until with the battle of Warsaw (July 28–30, 1656) Brandenburg took its place in the front rank of the military powers of Europe, and the treaty of Wehlau (Pacta Wehlawiensia, September 29, 1657) guaranteed the elector's sovereignty in Prussia. Terrible times of war recurred. The south of the country was so greatly depopulated that subsequently Sudauen and Galindien were repeopled by a mass immigration of Polish and Lithuanian workers—which historians have for the most part overlooked. The ruler understood his new dignity quite in the spirit of this period of autocracy. Some of the Prussians were still too stiff-necked to bow their heads willingly; but, after a severe contest, necessity compelled their acceptance of an unlimited monarchy. Prussia and Cleve, Brandenburg and Minden were henceforward the members of a unified German State. And lo when the Elector drove the Swedes in a wild rout across the ice on the Frisches Haff and as far as the walls of Riga, the Prussian peasants voluntarily took up arms and carried on a guerrilla war against the foe of the Empire. Many might curse the iron discipline of the autocrat, but happier days had dawned, and this people had once more a fatherland.

Even during the worst days experienced by this frontier people, the German spirit had continued to flicker amid the embers. To the generation of those who were brutalized by the great war, Simon Dach (1605–1659) sang of the cordial effects which pure and sincere love could have; and a century later, in the time of Hamann, Herder, and Kant, Prussia enjoyed a reputation for intellectual achievements which had never been hers during the rule of the Teutonic Knights. When the royal black eagle of Prussia rose above the red eagle of Brandenburg, and the remote province became more and more intimately associated with the fatherland, Prussia enjoyed a splendid turn of fortune, a genuine "ritornar al segno" such as Machiavelli had extolled as the salvation of a State. Then once more, as in the most flourishing period of the Order, did the well-rounded unity of Prussia contrast most favourably with the anarchy that prevailed in Poland, and the kings of the former land were well able to safeguard their co-religionists in the latter against the violence of the Jesuits.

Frederick the Great had in fine realized the Order's ancient plan of partition. This was the "first partition of Poland", when the heritage of which they had been robbed was restored to our people. On September 14, 1772, General Thadden stood by the gate of Marienburg at the head of the Sydow regiment and himself raised the barrier. On September 27th the estates of Prussia assembled in the conventual refectory of the fortress to pay homage to the German monarch. It would be most edifying if we could describe how across the centuries King Frederick was stretching his hands to Plauen and Kniprode and presenting himself to them as the saviour of the German civilization they had introduced so long ago. Indeed we can hardly doubt that he must have had some inkling of the profound historical significance of the reconquest of West Prussia. For in youth, when writing his *Mémoires pour servir à l'histoire de Brandenbourg,* he had severely stigmatized the disgrace that had been suffered by the Teutonic Knights, while the medal that was struck to commemorate the homage paid him at Marienburg bore the highly suggestive inscription: "regno redinte-grato praestata fides." But the writings penned in his old age show plainly enough that he primarily regarded the new province as the granary of the north, the water-way of the Vistula, and the necessary link between Pomerania and East Prussia; and that he would not have despised this welcome loot even if it had always been Slav territory. Moreover the official justification of the partition makes no mention of the Order, speak-ing only of the hereditary claim of Brandenburg to Pomerellen. How little understanding there was, in these days of the Enlightenment, for the romantic greatness of the Ordensland, is plainly shown by the way in which the maltreatment of the castle of Marien-burg persisted under Frederick's rule. We must, there-fore, guard against ascribing to him an awareness of nationalism which would have been foreign to his century. Let us be gratified, rather, that, thanks to a fruitful necessity, the king of Prussia was infallibly induced to fulfil his German mission, even though his conscious motive was furnished by a cold calculation of his own advantages.

The ambiguous reasons for the acquisition of this territory have long since been outweighed by the worthy use that was made of it. The half extinct sparks of Germanism were successfully fanned into flame under

Prussian rule, and since then West Prussia has been ours by the most sacred right, for whatever has thriven there in the way of justice and prosperity, of culture and humanity, has been wrought by German hands. Again could Königsberg congratulate itself on having within its walls the transient court of a hard-pressed Hohenzollern; again, though even more splendidly than in the days of the Great Elector, did the tottering State derive fresh energy from the love of its people. That very Königsberg diet which in former days had often appealed to the Poles for help against its own German princes, now ventured to command the first deed of our war of liberation; and the black cross of the militiaman was decked with finer garlands than those which of yore had adorned the black cross of the Teutonic Knight. New Germany sprung from the Middle Ages could gratefully repay to the motherland the old benefit.

Like an echo from those strenuous days there now began, with the assistance of funds supplied by all Germany, the rebuilding of the fortress of Marienburg. This gives a valuable hint to the historian, who, from the historical yearnings that have dominated an epoch can confidently divine its innermost secrets. Indeed, as if to spite the gloomy despair and mendacity of those who insist that our age has lost the creative spirit, opposite the restored fortress to-day the controlled river

is spanned by the bridges of Dirschau and Marienburg
—typically modern achievements. Beyond question
new life has awakened in this border world. No doubt
a drop of the old Lizard poison is still flowing in the
blood of a population difficult to guide and harsh in
its judgments; nevertheless in the party struggles of the
nineteenth century the self-assertive rationalism of Old
Prussia has always formed a valuable counterpoise to
the powers of conservatism. The first burgrave of the
restored stronghold was Heinrich Theodor von Schön,
the liberal Kantian.

It would not become Prussia to plume itself unduly
upon its present good fortune. The treasures of the
province have by no means yet been adequately
exploited. The prosperity which the country knew
before the days of Tannenberg has never been regained.
Its trade is still hampered by the embargoes of its
neighbour. All the same we can gladly bear in mind
how the long-winded activities of many generations
have saved this valuable country from the general
shipwreck of German colonies. Day by day Germans
are still carrying the advantages of civilization to the
east. But where the Slavs hold sway the German
teacher is usually received as an audacious intruder.
Only in Prussia has he remained a fully equipped
citizen and a master of the land which his ancestors
opened to civilization. After centuries this border

country re-entered the community of the German nation, to become more closely intertwined than ever with the great fatherland. Just as of old the conjoined energies of the Teutonic Knights and of the Osterlings carried the fame of the Germans far to the east, so to-day (a happy omen) are the united colours of Prussia and the Hanseatic League represented in the banner of our new realm. The military and the civil forces of the German nation have again entered into a firm alliance, never (D.V.) to be broken, and the Imperial Eagle which, through the storms of the ages, continued to wave undismayed over the forces that championed it in the distant Mark, has once again spread its pinions dominantly over German soil. He must indeed be a dullard whom the contemplation of this troubled but unceasing metamorphosis fails to inspire with the most ardent convictions. Let us encourage ourselves with history's greatest blessing, the freedom of that clear vision which enables us, amid the vicissitudes, the follies, and the sins of the moment, to recognize the inalterable dominion of world-constructing laws.

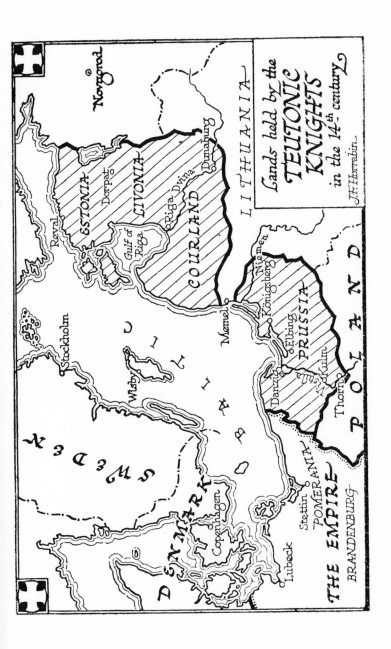

Lands held by the
TEUTONIC
KNIGHTS
in the 14th century
J.F.Horrabin